S0-ARJ-324

This New Perspectives
Second Edition
Reserved 2012 right page

INNOVATIVE TECHNOLOGIES

NUCLEAR ENERGY

ABDO
Publishing Company

Medway Public Library
26 High Street
Medway, MA 02053

INNOVATIVE TECHNOLOGIES

NUCLEAR ENERGY

BY MARCIA AMIDON LUSTED

CONTENT CONSULTANT

Paul P. H. Wilson

Associate Professor, Engineering Physics

Chair, Energy Analysis & Policy Program

University of Wisconsin–Madison

CREDITS

Published by ABDO Publishing Company, PO Box 398166, Minneapolis, MN 55439. Copyright © 2013 by Abdo Consulting Group, Inc. International copyrights reserved in all countries. No part of this book may be reproduced in any form without written permission from the publisher. The Essential Library™ is a trademark and logo of ABDO Publishing Company.

Printed in the United States of America,
North Mankato, Minnesota

102012
102013

 THIS BOOK CONTAINS AT LEAST 10% RECYCLED MATERIALS.

Editor: Rebecca Felix
Series Designer: Craig Hinton

Photo Credits: Martin Muránsky/Bigstock, cover; Fotolia, 6; Red Line Editorial, 8, 9, 35, 58–59; Mark Smith/Shutterstock Images, 11; Uwe Lein/APN/AP Images, 12; Shutterstock Images, 15, 32; Keystone-France/Gamma-Keystone/Getty Images, 16; US Air Force/AP Images, 19; Bettmann/Corbis/AP Images, 21, 51; Keystone/Hulton Archive/Getty Images, 27; Jeffrey Collins/AP Images, 30; Yoshikazu Tsuno/AFP/Getty Images, 39; The Yomiuri Shimbun/AP Images, 40; AP Images, 43, 74; Andrea Danti/Shutterstock Images, 46; Pavel Kosek/Shutterstock Images, 49; Dries Lauwers/iStockphoto, 54; Vanderlei Almeida/AFP/Getty Images, 63; John Miller/AP Images, 64; Virginia Postic/AP Images, 66; Shawn Rocco/AP Images, 69; Charles Dharapak/AP Images, 73; Koji Sasahara/AP Images, 78; Boris Horvat/AFP/Getty Images, 80; Emory Kristof/National Geographic/Getty Images, 84; Douglas C. Pizac/AP Images, 86; David Goldman/AP Images, 88; iStockphoto, 90, 100; Itsuo Inouye/AP Images, 93; Imaginechina/AP Images, 96

Library of Congress Cataloging-in-Publication Data
Lusted, Marcia Amidon.
  Nuclear energy / Marcia Amidon Lusted.
    p. cm. -- (Innovative technologies)
Audience: 11-18.
Includes bibliographical references.
ISBN 978-1-61783-466-0
1. Nuclear energy--Juvenile literature. I. Title.
TK9148.L87 2013
621.48'3--dc23
                              2012024011

>> TABLE OF CONTENTS

CHAPTER 1
NUCLEAR ENERGY AT A GLANCE 6

CHAPTER 2
THE HISTORY OF NUCLEAR ENERGY 16

CHAPTER 3
RADIATION 32

CHAPTER 4
CREATING NUCLEAR ENERGY 46

CHAPTER 5
NUCLEAR PLANTS AND REACTORS 54

CHAPTER 6
NUCLEAR WASTE 66

CHAPTER 7
THE BENEFITS OF NUCLEAR POWER 80

CHAPTER 8
A FRESH LOOK 90

Glossary 102

Additional Resources 104

Source Notes 106

Index 110

About the Author 112

About the Content Consultant 112

CHAPTER 1

NUCLEAR ENERGY AT A GLANCE

According to the *2011 World Energy Outlook Factsheet*, the world's demand for energy will increase by one-third between 2010 and 2035, and energy-related carbon dioxide emissions will increase by 20 percent.[1] Climate change and the creation of greenhouse gas emissions, such as carbon, that contribute to it are becoming even more of an issue. The world is becoming more and more aware of climate change and carbon emissions. Countries including the United States are experiencing increasing prices for gasoline and home heating oil. It is imperative the world finds alternatives, such as nuclear power, to supplement energy needs.

As of 2012, there were 441 nuclear power plants worldwide, which supplied approximately 16 percent of the world's electricity.[2] One hundred and four nuclear power plants operate to produce roughly 20 percent of the electricity used in the

« **As concerns rise over energy production, alternatives such as nuclear power are being given more consideration.**

United States.[3] These nuclear plants are not all the same type, but each one operates with the same basic process: using uranium ore that has been processed into fuel to create a nuclear reaction that ultimately produces electricity.

Using nuclear energy is an alternative to burning fossil fuels to create the power that heats and provides electricity to homes, businesses, and entire communities. Fossil fuels are

US NUCLEAR POWER PLANTS

Source: US Nuclear Regulatory Commission, as of 2010

substances that take millions of years to form in nature. These fuels include coal, oil, and natural gas, which are all commonly used as sources of energy. All energy sources have pros and cons. But there is increasing concern about the challenges posed by using fossil fuels. When burned, fossil fuels create greenhouse gas emissions that damage the environment and contribute to climate change.

For many countries, including the United States, relying on fossil fuel energy also makes them dependent on foreign countries that have an abundance of the needed fuel. US politicians and the government are increasingly concerned about this dependency on foreign countries for oil. The need to acquire or insure continued supplies of oil can lead to complicated political situations and even wars. As the urgency for

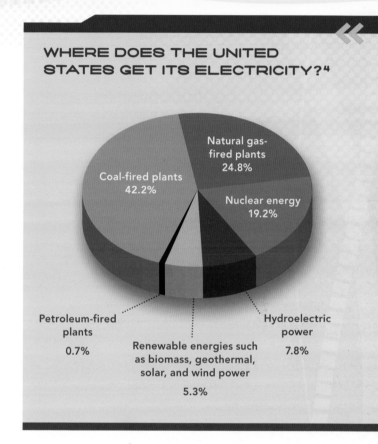

WHERE DOES THE UNITED STATES GET ITS ELECTRICITY?[4]

Natural gas-fired plants 24.8%

Coal-fired plants 42.2%

Nuclear energy 19.2%

Petroleum-fired plants 0.7%

Renewable energies such as biomass, geothermal, solar, and wind power 5.3%

Hydroelectric power 7.8%

countries to independently support their energy use and preventing further environmental damage worldwide increases, many researchers and scientists are busily seeking alternatives.

One advantage of nuclear power for many countries is that the uranium most commonly used to create it can be found and mined in their own countries. Nuclear power also provides more energy, relative to the mass of its fuel source, than fossil fuels. According to the Idaho National Laboratory, "Just one uranium fuel pellet—roughly the size of the tip of an adult's little finger—contains the same amount of energy as 17,000 cubic feet of natural gas, 1,780 pounds of coal, or 149 gallons of oil."[5]

ZERO EMISSIONS TECHNOLOGY

How does nuclear energy measure up to other forms of energy in emissions? According to a congressional study in 2008, "Coal burning technologies emit the most carbon dioxide per unit of electricity; natural gas technologies emit carbon dioxide at about half that rate; and nuclear power, a 'zero emissions technology,' emits no carbon dioxide at all."[6]

Nuclear energy is created from a process called nuclear fission, in which unstable atoms in an element, most commonly uranium, break up and release heat. The nuclear fission process does not combust fuels that result in greenhouse gases. Instead, the byproducts of nuclear power, which are radioactive fission products, stay trapped inside the nuclear fuel.

If fossil fuel power plants were to replace the existing nuclear power plants providing electricity worldwide, the amount of carbon dioxide emitted would greatly increase.

Although nuclear energy has many advantages, the radioactive materials created as a byproduct of nuclear fission are cause of great concern for many. Overexposure to radioactive materials can be extremely dangerous to people and the environment. Radioactivity is found within a nuclear reactor, where the energy is created, and is also in the waste leftover from the process. This waste takes thousands of years to break down, making the threat of radioactivity leaking from the spent nuclear fuel if not contained properly or through an accident, a serious issue. These issues have incited much debate over nuclear energy since its earliest uses. Nuclear energy is not a new discovery. It started out as a form of energy with great promise in the 1950s, and many nuclear power plants were constructed. Then much public opinion shifted against nuclear energy over the next few decades after several high-profile nuclear power plant accidents involving radioactive materials occurred.

But now that the world is facing shortages of fossil fuels and the threat of climate change from greenhouse gases, nuclear energy is once again receiving serious consideration. New types of nuclear plants are being explored and developed, and public opinion of nuclear energy is rising as a preferred source. According to an annual survey conducted by the Nuclear Energy Institute (NEI) in 2012, 64 percent of those surveyed were in favor of nuclear energy.[7] However, safety standards, accident prevention and management, public fears of meltdowns or other

An aerial view deep inside a nuclear reactor, where radiation is created as a byproduct of fission

catastrophes, and storage of radioactive nuclear waste remain important aspects that must be addressed when considering nuclear power as a key energy source.

Researchers are working to address these issues in hopes of making nuclear energy a viable option to help decrease the world's dependence on fossil fuel energy. Innovations aiming to resolve these issues may be the answer to nuclear energy rising to a bright future from a turbulent past.

Many researchers believe **nuclear power is a viable option for powerful, clean energy in the future.**

CHAPTER 2

THE HISTORY OF NUCLEAR ENERGY

Nuclear energy required considerable scientific experimentation and development before it came to be used as a way to generate electricity. Uranium, a main fuel source for nuclear energy, was discovered in 1789. Radiation, which is emitted by uranium, was discovered and studied in the late nineteenth century. Scientists also studied atoms, the particles making up all matter, and discovered the three components in an atom: neutrons, protons, and electrons. They also gradually discovered how to make these atomic components split. In 1934, Italian physicist Enrico Fermi discovered how to bombard the nucleus of an atom with neutrons, creating large amounts of energy and heat in a process called fission. Most research into nuclear fission then occurred in the early 1940s, when governments developed the technology for atomic weapons.

 Enrico Fermi in his laboratory in 1935

THE MANHATTAN PROJECT

In 1941, the United States entered into World War II (1939–1945), siding with the Allies against the Axis powers that included Japan, Italy, and Germany. The US government began studying nuclear fission at this time. The enormous amount of energy released during fission could be used as a destructive force in an atomic bomb. In September 1942, the US Army established the Manhattan Project, which would supervise the development of an atomic bomb. This project was spurred on by information that Germany was already six months ahead of the Allied forces in constructing an atomic bomb.

The Manhattan Project cost $2 billion, approximately $25 billion in today's dollars, and involved the work of both military and civilian scientists.[1] The project was top secret, even though more than 130,000 people were involved. To ensure secrecy for the project, only a small group of privileged officials and scientists were made aware that an atomic bomb was being developed. The project culminated in the development of two bombs, which were deployed in August of 1945 with Japan as the target. "Little Boy," the nuclear bomb dropped on Hiroshima, Japan, on August 6, had a force equal to 20,000 short tons (approximately 18,000 metric tons) of TNT.[2] "Fat Man," a nuclear bomb with the same power, was dropped on Nagasaki, Japan, three days later.[3] These powerful bombs caused major destruction in Nagasaki and Hiroshima. The force alone of the bomb in Hiroshima could be felt for 37 miles (60 km).[4] Injury and illness

Smoke from the powerful atomic bomb Little Boy rising over Hiroshima on August 6, 1945

from radiation exposure plagued survivors of the initial explosions. An exact amount has been hard to estimate, but it is believed that approximately 150,000 deaths occurred from these bombings combined.[5] The power of nuclear fission was made clear to all.

The devastation of these atomic bombs created worldwide turmoil for a long time afterward. These events also sparked an arms race between the United States and what was then the Soviet Union. Both countries concentrated on building up extensive arsenals of nuclear weapons during a period of time known as the Cold War.

THE PEACEFUL ATOM

Nuclear energy may have been initially developed mainly for military weapons, but even in its earliest days people were interested in developing peaceful uses as well. As the government was concentrating on World War II in 1945, nuclear physicist Alvin Weinberg told the US Senate's Special Committee on Atomic Energy, "Atomic power can cure as well as kill. It can fertilize and enrich a region as well as devastate it. It can widen man's horizons as well as force him back into the cave."[6] In 1946, the US Congress established the Atomic Energy Commission (AEC) as part of the Atomic Energy Act to regulate and ensure the safety of nuclear energy.

Scientists began developing other uses for nuclear power. In 1946, *Newsweek* magazine cited a few examples for peaceful civilian uses: atomic-powered airplanes, rockets, and even automobiles. It went on to say that large electric generating stations and small power plants for the home were likely. There was even speculation that tiny atomic generators would be wired to clothing to keep a person cool in summer and warm in winter.[7] During nuclear energy's developmental years, scientists also came up with the idea of a nuclear boiler, using the heat produced from nuclear fission to boil water and produce steam. It would be the basis for developing nuclear power plants.

President Eisenhower
giving his speech
promoting peaceful
nuclear energy use on
December 8, 1953

The military also began looking into less destructive uses for nuclear power during World War II. In 1946, the US Army Air Force initiated projects researching nuclear propulsion, or using nuclear energy for transportation. Many years of nuclear propulsion research followed. On January 21, 1954, the first military nuclear-powered submarine, the USS *Nautilus*, was launched. Reactors used in nuclear propulsion can run for a long time before they need to be refueled, allowing ships to be at sea for long periods of time.

As the military sought alternatives to using nuclear energy as a weapon, finding nonmilitary nuclear uses also remained a focus politically. President Dwight D. Eisenhower made a famous speech before the United Nations General Assembly on December 8, 1953:

The United States knows that if the fearful trend of atomic military build-up can be reversed, this greatest of destructive forces can be developed into a great boon, for the benefit of all mankind. The United States knows that peaceful power from atomic energy is no dream of the future. The capability, already proved, is here today.[7]

This speech became known as the Atoms for Peace speech. It marked the beginning of a new era of nuclear energy for peaceful civilian purposes.

Congress replaced a law that made the AEC responsible for regulating nuclear energy in 1946 with the new Atomic Energy Act of 1954, which would make it possible to develop nuclear power as a commercial industry, rather than a government-run one. The AEC wanted to ensure the public was safe from nuclear power hazards without having to impose so many restrictions that the industry would suffer. As US scientists and engineers worked to develop nuclear power technology, the world's first commercial nuclear power plant was successfully constructed and operated in the Soviet Union in 1954.

INTERNATIONAL ATOMIC ENERGY AGENCY

As part of the United Nations' Atoms for Peace organization, the International Atomic Energy Agency (IAEA) was set up to promote worldwide peaceful uses of nuclear energy that incorporate safety and security, science and technology, and safeguards and verification.

The IAEA monitors nuclear safety around the world, helping with construction and management of nuclear power plants. The IAEA also aims to help countries, particularly those with limited resources, use nuclear energy for developing agriculture, water-resource management, and industry. It is dedicated to stopping the spread of nuclear weapons around the world and helping countries focus on positive uses of nuclear energy rather than destructive ones.

THE RISE AND FALL OF NUCLEAR PLANTS

In 1957, the United States opened its first nuclear power plant in Shippingport, Pennsylvania. Shippingport was the beginning of a boom in the construction of nuclear power plants, which can take up to 12 years to build.[8] By 1987, 104 nuclear power plants were constructed and put into operation around the country. Although the industry was booming, many people were skeptical about the safety of the buildings and the adequacy of the processes within. Critics of nuclear power plants became vocal throughout the 1960s. They claimed the AEC's regulations were not strict enough, especially in areas such as radiation protection, reactor safety, choosing sites for new plants, and protection of the environment.

DISNEY'S "OUR FRIEND THE ATOM"

In 1955, Walt Disney built a new exhibit in the Tomorrowland section of the Disneyland theme park in California. It was called "Our Friend the Atom" and spotlighted nuclear energy in a cheerful way, discussing nondestructive uses as well as the history of atomic energy. Disney also produced a short film and companion children's book of the same name for the government. The film talked about atomic energy as a genie in a bottle, capable of both good and evil, which mankind was to control. Many children were shown the film in school.

But an energy crisis in the 1970s fueled nuclear power plant construction despite any opposition that existed. During the crisis, domestic oil production could no longer keep up with demand and brought with it shortages of electricity and gasoline. Then the United States took sides during an ongoing conflict between nations in the Middle East that led to an embargo in which foreign countries limited the amount of oil they would ship to the United States. Power brownouts, where power is reduced but not cut off completely, and gas shortages, creating long lines at gas stations, also occurred. Unlike gasoline, which did not have enough availability domestically to support the country's energy needs, nuclear energy was a source that could be completely generated in the United States, using fuel mined within the country. Utility companies began constructing nuclear power plants at an increasing rate starting in the 1970s. They saw nuclear energy as a relatively cheap and clean way to produce electricity.

UNION OF CONCERNED SCIENTISTS

One of the most vocal critics of atomic energy is the Union of Concerned Scientists, which was formed at the Massachusetts Institute of Technology in 1969, and still exists today. It was originally created to protest using scientific research for military purposes and promote using scientific research for the public's interest. It has addressed issues such as climate change, space debris, and missile defense systems. It has also voiced concern over the effects of nuclear technology on society, the destructive potential of nuclear weapons, and what it believes are design flaws in nuclear power plants.

By the late 1970s, however, construction had come to a virtual halt. The energy crisis in the early 1970s had inspired improved energy efficiency practices and in 1978, the National Energy Conservation Act was put in effect. The act created incentives for reduced energy consumption including government grants for public facilities such as schools and hospitals to practice energy reduction. Energy demand waned, and along with it, nuclear power plant construction.

The US Nuclear Regulatory Commission (NRC) was established during the boom of nuclear power-plant construction in the 1970s. It would take the place of the AEC, which continued receiving criticism that its regulations were not strict enough. The NRC took a close look at nuclear reactors and created a series of requirements to help prevent a major nuclear accident, especially one that might release huge amounts of radiation from a plant into populated areas.

ACCIDENTS

Even under strict regulation, however, nuclear power plants were subject to accidents. Two significant accidents in 1979 and 1986 created safety fears that further hindered future nuclear plant construction. On March 28, 1979, a mechanical failure at the nuclear power plant Three Mile Island in Pennsylvania caused the reactor's feedwater pumps to stop working. These were the pumps that provided cooling water to the reactor where fission occurred. The reactor shut down automatically, but the valve remained open and allowed cooling water, needed in the reactor to keep the core of the reactor cool, to continue draining from the reactor. The core of the reactor overheated and the nuclear fuel core began to melt down. Although a serious accident did take place, the plant operators made sure cooling water was pumped back into the reactor. The plant's systems also kept a more catastrophic accident from taking place by shutting down the reactor immediately so radiation would not vent to other parts of the plant. Radioactive material was released from the plant, and preschool-aged children and pregnant women were evacuated in areas within a five-mile (8 km) radius of the plant, but it was only a precaution. No recorded human health effects, injuries, or deaths resulted from the accident.[9] Despite this, the Three Mile Island accident caused many people to take a closer look at nuclear energy at a time when new plants had been built at a steady rate. The accident incited much discussion and several protests.

After the incident, the NRC evaluated emergency planning, response, and communication practices and found there was room for improvement. According to the NRC, although it was the most serious US nuclear accident to date,

It brought about sweeping changes involving emergency response planning, reactor operator training, human factors engineering, radiation protection, and many other

After the accident at Three Mile Island, people staged protests.

areas of nuclear power plant operations. It also caused the US Nuclear Regulatory Commission to tighten and heighten its regulatory oversight.[10]

Then on April 26, 1986, another accident took place, this time at the Chernobyl nuclear power plant in what was then the Soviet Union and is now Ukraine. The Chernobyl plant was a type of plant not constructed in the United States because of safety concerns in its design. It was also poorly regulated with insufficient safety practices and training for its workers. The accident occurred when a sudden surge of power at the plant caused an explosion. Plant operators had been conducting a test and so had disabled safety systems for it that might have prevented the explosion. The explosion destroyed part of the reactor and released huge amounts of radioactive material into the atmosphere that drifted for hundreds of miles, all the way into other countries.[11] The reactor itself and surrounding buildings burned for days. Many of the plant's workers and people who lived nearby suffered from radiation-related sicknesses.[12] Many of the firefighters who came to the scene later died of radiation poisoning.[13]

NUCLEAR PLANT PROTESTS

For almost as long as utilities have been building nuclear plants in the United States, people have expressed concerns about them by organizing and demonstrating against them. One of the most famous groups was the Clamshell Alliance, which formed in Rye, New Hampshire, in July of 1976. Its purpose was to protest the construction of the Seabrook Nuclear Power Plant. The group got its name from the clam beds in the Seabrook area, which local fishermen feared would be destroyed by building the nuclear plant there and possible warm water discharging into the ocean. The Clamshell Alliance practiced civil disobedience, occupying various sites using nonviolent techniques. The plant was constructed in 1970s into the 1980s. It gained its license to operate in 1990, and it still operates today.

While there had already been some antinuclear demonstrations in the United States during this time, these two incidents turned public US opinion against nuclear power. The scope of the Chernobyl accident also made nuclear power less attractive to much of the world in general.

Developers were also looking at tremendous price tags associated with constructing new nuclear power plants due to safety equipment, training, and regulations and licensing needed. These costs are a primary reason why no new nuclear plants were built in the United States for more than 30 years. Existing plants did continue to produce energy, but others were decommissioned and no longer used.

Only since the early 2000s, in the face of increasingly dwindling fossil fuel supplies and the fears concerning greenhouse gases and climate change, have utilities begun to develop new plant designs and proposals. But even as the government and utilities consider a new era of nuclear power, debates over the pros and cons of this form of electricity generation continue.

Another significant nuclear accident in 2011 raised concerns yet again. The accident was triggered when an earthquake and tsunami struck near the Fukushima prefecture in Japan on March 11, 2011. These natural disasters damaged the Fukushima Daiichi nuclear power plant, flooding emergency generators at the plant and making it impossible to run coolant pumps that kept the reactors from overheating. A subsequent explosion damaged the reactor building

and exposed the spent fuel pools where radioactive fuel was stored. Unlike Three Mile Island and Chernobyl, the incident involved multiple reactors: a total of six reactors were damaged. Evacuations of more than 100,000 people in the surrounding area were necessary. Due to the evacuation, as of August 2012 there were no reported instances of death or radiation sickness relating to the accident.[14] Although concerns rose after this recent accident, nuclear power's worth as an energy source remained apparent. In February 2012, the NRC approved construction of two new reactors in Georgia. One month later, it approved construction of two more in South Carolina. By August, however, complications at a nuclear plant in Pennsylvania led the NRC to put a hold on any additional requests for new construction.

High-profile accidents and nuclear power's war-related history create complex considerations when looking to its future use as an energy source. The two major areas of concern are the possible exposure to radiation from either a power plant accident or from the stored radioactive waste created from nuclear energy production. Innovators are working on technological advances to address these problems, including a new generation of high-performance computers that use models to predict situations and avoid radioactive catastrophes. But what exactly is radiation, and why is radioactive waste such a big challenge?

Construction preparation in April 2012 for one of the two reactors to be built at V.C. Summer Nuclear Power Station in Jenkinsville, South Carolina

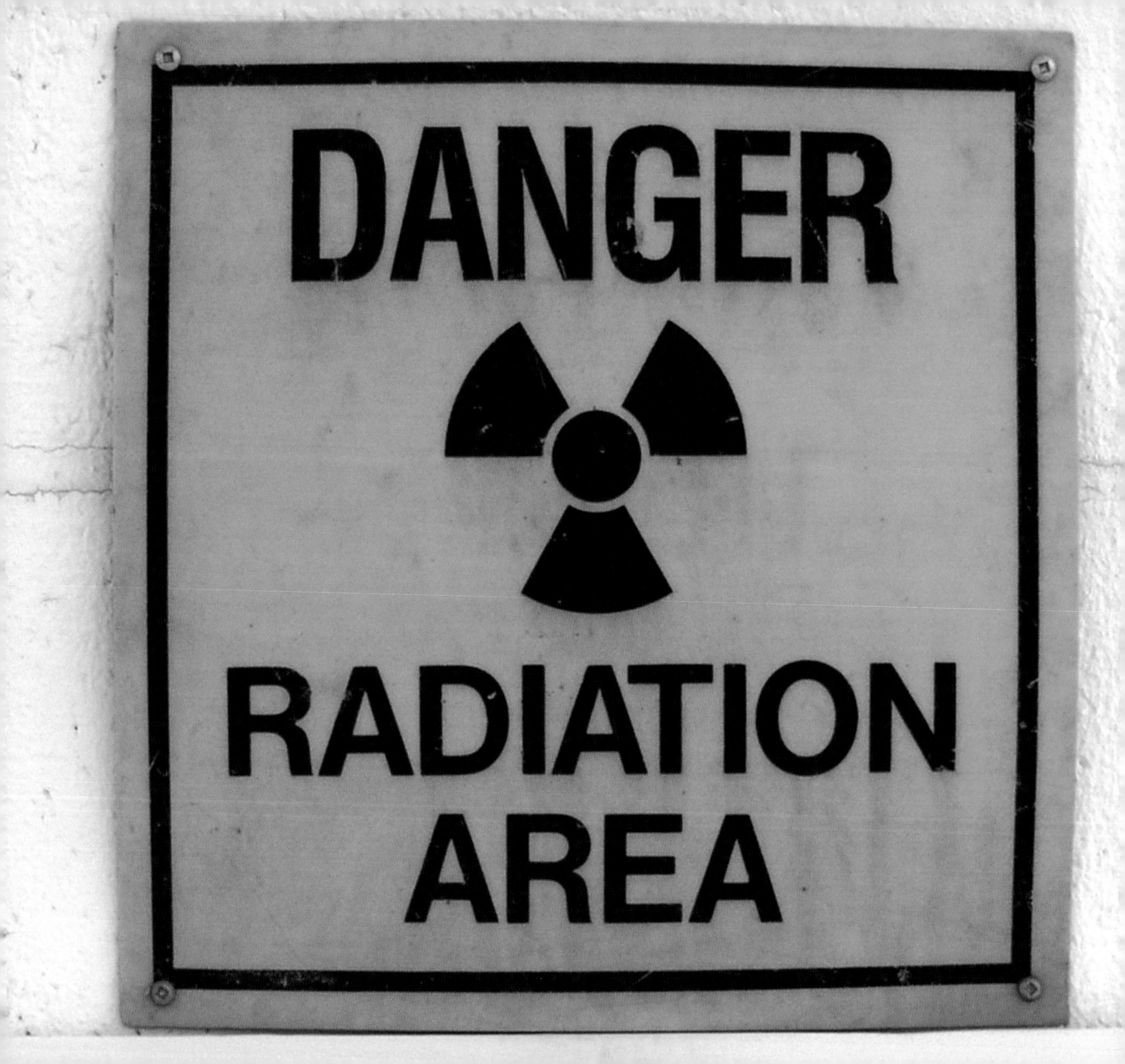
DANGER
RADIATION
AREA

RADIATION

When people think of nuclear energy, their biggest concern often is radiation. Radiation has existed in nature for millions of years. It is not visible to the naked eye, it cannot be smelled, felt, or tasted, and yet it can be deadly. But not all kinds of radiation are the same, nor is every kind harmful.

WHAT IS RADIOACTIVITY?

Radioactivity is the emission of energetic particles created when the nuclei in atoms of certain radioactive materials break down. Fission is just one of many processes that emits radiation, and it is a process used to create nuclear energy. Radiation emitted during this process can interact with other atoms and have a negative effect on people and the environment. However, radioactive material is naturally present in food, soil, water, and air in small amounts. Radiation is present all around us, emitted from these

« A label featuring the trefoil, the universal symbol for radiation, must be included on all radioactive devices, materials, and areas.

things as well as from space. It is only when the amount of radiation is highly concentrated that it becomes dangerous. Radiation and radioactivity have been studied since the nineteenth century, and by the time nuclear power began being used to create energy in the 1950s, radioactivity was well understood by scientists.

There are four different types of radiation, and each one can affect the human body in a different way. All radiation can cause cells to mutate or become damaged. Alpha particles cause skin to redden but do not penetrate very deep. However, if the radioactive material that emits alpha particles is inhaled they can cause lung cancer. Because alpha particles don't penetrate far, they need to get inside your body to do damage. Beta particles are stronger and can travel through the skin but do not penetrate internal organs. Gamma rays and X-rays can damage the whole body because they can penetrate more deeply. The risk of developing cancer from these is higher than from other types. Neutron rays are the most dangerous radiated rays, because they can most easily penetrate the human body. The two types of radiation emitted during nuclear fission are gamma and neutron, but radioactive fission products will, together, emit a combination of all four types.

However, despite risk being present, scientists and doctors are not entirely sure just how dangerous low doses can be in regard to causing cancer. Cancers caused by radiation may take years to develop, and the likelihood of developing cancer depends on the amount and type of

All types of radiation penetrate human skin. As depicted, neutron radiation is strongest, able to penetrate concrete.

TYPES AND PENETRATION LEVELS OF RADIATION

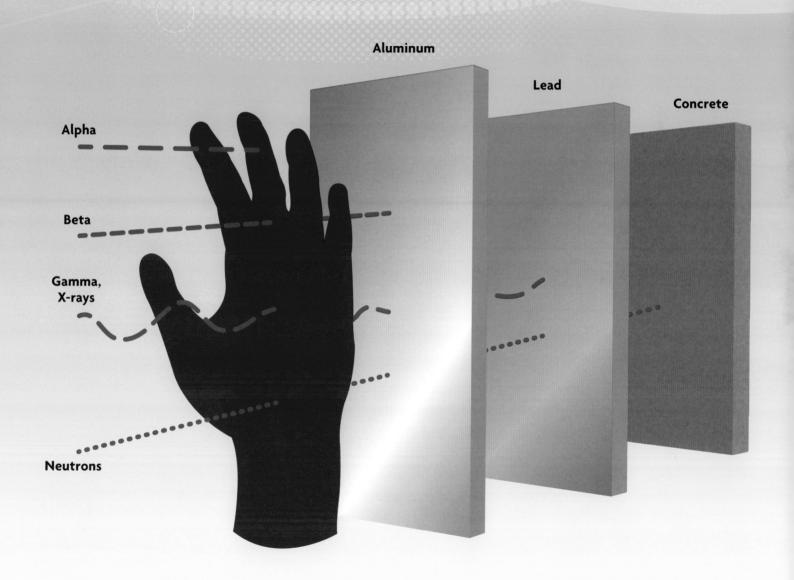

Aluminum

Lead

Concrete

Alpha

Beta

Gamma,
X-rays

Neutrons

MEASURING RADIATION

Radiation is measured in many ways. According to the Centers for Disease Control: "Different units of measure are used depending on which aspect of radiation is being measured. For example, the amount of radiation being given off, or emitted, by a radioactive material is measured using the conventional unit curie (Ci), named for the famed scientist Marie Curie, or the SI unit Becquerel (Bq). The radiation dose absorbed by a person (that is, the amount of energy deposited in human tissue by radiation) is measured using the conventional unit rad or the SI unit gray (Gy). The biological risk of exposure to radiation (that is, the risk that a person will suffer health effects from an exposure to radiation) is measured using the conventional unit rem or the SI unit sievert (Sv)."[2]

radiation received. It is easier for scientists to see the effects of high doses of radiation. These are called "deterministic effects" because they are directly determined by how much radiation the patient received: the higher the dose received, the greater the symptoms in the human body.[1] One of the first deterministic effects is radiation sickness, which results in symptoms of nausea and vomiting. Diarrhea, loss of hair, and body hemorrhaging that damages the immune system and leaves the patient vulnerable to infection are also effects.

Some argue that the amount of radiation a person encounters throughout a typical day is high, but that chances of developing cancer or disease from it are slim. According to Dr. Bernard L. Cohen at the University of Pittsburgh:

Radiation occurs naturally in our environment; a typical person is and always has been struck by 15,000 particles of radiation every second from natural sources, and an average medical x-ray involves being struck by 100 billion. While this might seem to be very dangerous, it is not, because the probability for a particle of radiation entering a human body to cause a cancer or a genetic disease is only one chance in 30 million billion (30 quintillion).[3]

Still, however small a chance, some take a precautionary stance. According to the American Cancer Society Web site,

> Most scientists and regulatory agencies agree that even small doses of ionizing radiation increase cancer risk, although by a very small amount. In general, the risk of cancer from radiation exposure increases as the dose of radiation increases.[4]

BANANA RADIATION

One of the more informal methods of measuring radiation exposure is called the Banana Equivalent Dose. The scale compares the amount of radiation exposure from a significant event, such as the Chernobyl disaster or the events at the Fukushima Daichi nuclear plant in Japan, to the amount of natural radiation the average person receives simply from eating a banana. Bananas are rich in potassium, which is naturally radioactive. For example, living within 50 miles (80 km) of a nuclear power plant for one year will give a person approximately the same amount of radiation exposure as eating one banana. One dental X-ray will be 50 times as much radiation as eating one banana.[5]

FEAR FACTOR

Radiation is impossible to detect without equipment. Producing an undetectable byproduct that can be dangerous incurs fear when it comes to public opinion and nuclear power. Even after the fuel has been used in a nuclear plant to create fission, it is still highly radioactive. Eventually, spent nuclear fuel and other radioactive waste generated by a power plant will decay to safe levels, but this may take thousands of years.

Nuclear power plants are constructed to minimize the possibility of radiation escaping and harming people or the environment. For every system in a nuclear power plant that could possibly fail, there is a back-up system to limit how much damage can actually be done. Each back-up system also has a back-up system, so it takes a catastrophic failure of multiple systems before serious consequences take place. In the case of the Three Mile Island accident, two key pieces of equipment failed and human error made the situation worse. But the thick steel reactor vessel and the concrete containment building did their jobs and contained dangerous levels of radiation so that the public was not exposed. In contrast, the Chernobyl nuclear power plant in Russia did not have a containment building, which allowed dangerous radiation to escape and harm both workers and people living farther away from the plant.

Fear of radiation exposure is of great concern to many people, especially in the wake of a nuclear accident.

To prevent such harm, the NRC created standards for exposure to and handling of radioactive materials, providing a sufficient margin of safety for anyone working in those situations. Plant workers are strictly regulated and supervised to ensure that their dose of

≪

Nuclear power plant workers wear protective clothing and are often required to use dosimeters to measure their radiation exposure.

radiation does not exceed a certain safe lifetime limit. Workers wear different types of protective clothing, from gloves, shoe covers, goggles, and coveralls, to full-coverage anticontamination suits in extremely radioactive areas. Workers are sometimes required to have personal dosimeters, which are devices that keep track of the amount of radiation exposure they collect over time.

Residents living nearby need not worry about overexposure from living near a nuclear power plant, according to the NEI. It states the amount of radiation people living near a nuclear power

COMMON RADIATION DOSES

People are exposed to radiation daily from different sources, such as naturally occurring radioactive materials in the soil and cosmic rays from outer space, of which we receive more when we fly in an airplane. The average American absorbs approximately 620 millirems (6.2 mSv) per year. Half of this comes from natural sources and half from man-made sources.[7]

Sources of Exposure	Dose in rem	Dose in sievert (Sv)[8]
Cosmic rays during a round-trip airplane flight from New York to Los Angeles	3 mrem	0.03 mSv
One dental X-ray	4–15 mrem	0.04–0.15 mSv
One chest X-ray	10 mrem	0.1 mSv

The maximum exposure allowed for a nuclear power worker per year is 5,000 millirems (50 mSv).[9] With exposure that exceeds 10,000 millirems (100 mSv), the probability of cancer increases with the dose.[10]

plant are exposed to is "insignificant and is of no threat to the health of the public."[6] Leaked radioactive materials, however, can be dangerous. In addition to human sickness or death, leaked radioactivity can cause damage to the surrounding environment. The effects of radiation exposure on plants and animals can include damaging cells and then stunting new cell growth, mutations, and susceptibility to disease.

Since the terrorist attacks on the World Trade Center in New York City in September of 2001, there have also been increasing concerns over the safety of nuclear plant buildings themselves. Many fear terrorists could take over a nuclear plant and use it as a weapon or even crash an airliner into a nuclear plant and release catastrophic amounts of radioactivity. Plants that either enrich uranium for use as nuclear fuel, or reprocess spent fuel, would be sources of nuclear materials. Some fear more nuclear power plants and reprocessing plants might provide more opportunities for theft and terrorism. The NRC's responsibilities include the safety of nuclear materials, particularly as terrorism has become an increasing threat. They have created safeguards for nuclear materials including protection against possible theft or sabotage. The United States does not currently reprocess spent fuel, but engineering plants to adhere to all nuclear plant safety standards in general has added a great deal to the cost of constructing them. This often makes nuclear power plants too expensive for many utilities to construct and maintain.

New technologies for protecting humans from radiation are being developed. One current way to protect humans from gamma radiation is through thick lead shielding. A company called Radiation Shield Technologies in Medley, Florida, created a new material called Demron, which protects against radiation, heat, and chemicals.

Dan Edwards, the head of business development at Radiation Shield Technologies, wearing one of the company's Demron protective suits

USES OF RADIATION

Nuclear energy is used for many other purposes beside energy generation and weapons. Such uses include:

> radioactive materials being used in many occupations as industrial tools, gauges, and imaging machines.
> archaeologists using naturally occurring radioactive materials in carbon dating to determine the age of artifacts and fossils.
> X-rays and radiation treatments for cancer
> exposing foods to radiation to kill germs and preserve freshness
> using radioactive material in home smoke detectors.

Japanese plastics company Teijin Chemicals Limited developed a new kind of polyester resin plastic, called SCINTIREX, that becomes fluorescent when exposed to radiation. It can be used in radiation detection devices and will make them less expensive.

As research on radiation protection continues, the hazards are controversial—how much radiation is safe, and how much is dangerous?—and the set of standards is open to debate. Creating radioactivity as a byproduct is just one reason the process of creating nuclear power must be performed carefully. Each step in the entire nuclear energy creation process, from mining and processing the fuel, creating the reaction, and handling waste, must be thoroughly understood for safe and efficient production. Thorough knowledge of uranium and nuclear fission on an atomic level is an important first step.

RADIATION POWDER

Australian scientists from Queensland University of Technology are developing a type of powder that cleans radioactivity out of water. According to an article from the online British publication the *Register*, the powder "will clean the radioactive particles in a ton of water with a single gram, provided it's properly distributed or filtered."[11]

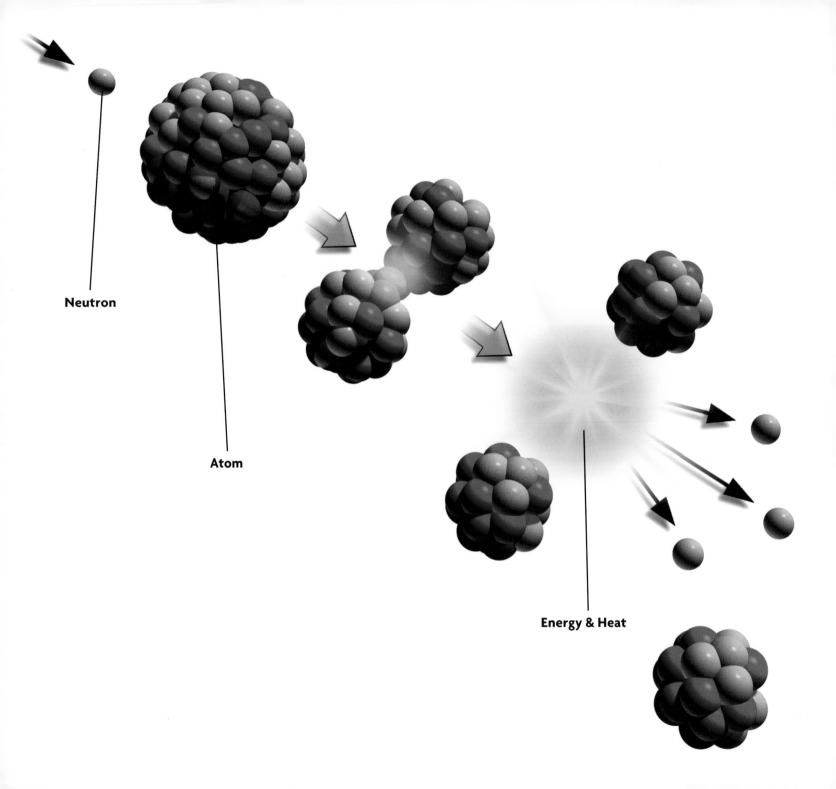

Neutron

Atom

Energy & Heat

CHAPTER 4

CREATING NUCLEAR ENERGY

C reating nuclear power begins with a process called fission, which takes place when atoms are split apart. All matter is made up of billions of atoms, which are tiny particles too small to be seen by the human eye. Each atom has a nucleus made up of protons and neutrons. In some kinds of atoms, this nucleus is unstable, or radioactive, and breaks up at a rapid pace. In some radioactive atoms, such as uranium, this breaking up emits neutrons as well as a large amount of heat. The neutrons then hit other atoms and make them split apart as well, creating even more neutrons and more heat in a chain reaction. This whole process is known as nuclear fission, and it is the basis for what takes place at a nuclear power plant to create nuclear power.

Uranium, a radioactive, natural heavy metal, is the fuel most often used to run a nuclear power plant. The state of uranium's nucleus after absorbing a neutron

« **During nuclear fission, a neutron hits an atom. The atom splits apart, and energy is released. Neutrons released hit other atoms to cause a chain reaction.**

URANIUM

Uranium is a nonrenewable resource, meaning there is only a limited amount in nature, as with fossil fuels. However, according to the US Department of Energy (DOE), uranium is forty-eighth on the list of the most abundant elements found in natural crustal rock, and 40 times more abundant than the element silver.[2] It is a very dense element, which means it has a high mass per unit volume. "For example, while a gallon of milk weighs about 8 pounds, a gallon container of uranium would weigh about 150 pounds," according to the DOE's Argonne National Laboratory Web site.[3]

Uranium occurs naturally in three isotopes, or different forms: U-234, U-235, and U-238. The difference between these isotopes is the amount of neutrons present in the nucleus. More than 99 percent of natural uranium is U-238; U-235 makes up less than 1 percent.[4] U-234 accounts for less than 0.01 percent.[5] The isotope U-235 works best in a nuclear reactor. Separating the U-235 from the U-238 to increase the concentration of U-235 is a process known as enrichment.

makes it ideal to create nuclear fission, releasing a large amount of heat and energy, as well as radioactivity. The fission of an atom of uranium creates approximately 10 million times more energy than the combustion, or burning, of an atom of carbon from coal.[1] Because of the sheer power involved, nuclear fission must be carefully controlled. And given the hazardous radioactive byproduct nuclear fission creates, the process must also be carefully contained.

The process of creating nuclear energy begins with mining the uranium in its raw form. Much of the uranium used in the United States' nuclear plants is imported. However, a small percent is mined domestically from places such as New Mexico, Wyoming, Utah, Nebraska, Colorado, Texas, and Arizona.

Inside a uranium ore mine »

Uranium is most commonly mined either underground or in open pits. Residual ground rock from the milling operation, which contains most of the radioactive materials, is discharged into what are called tailings dams. These dams hold residual solids to prevent any leaking of radioactive liquid. Once mined, the uranium is then sent to a mill where it is processed. This is where the raw uranium ore is crushed and the concentrated uranium is removed, leaving behind any extra materials. At this point the uranium is known as yellowcake because of its rough texture and yellowish-orange color. Then it is sent to a processing plant where the yellowcake is refined and enriched to become more concentrated. Because certain types of nuclear reactors require certain enrichments of uranium in order to operate properly, the fuel has to be processed to meet these requirements. There are two processing plants in the United States that are leased by the United States Enrichment Corporation from the US Department of Energy (DOE). One is in Kentucky still operating, and one is in Ohio and not in operation. A third US processing plant is in New Mexico and is privately owned and operated.

In the final step at a processing plant, the fuel is processed into small ceramic pellets the size of a pencil eraser. These pellets are, in turn, put into long metal tubes called fuel rods. Finally, the fuel rods are grouped into the fuel assemblies used in nuclear power plants. The fuel assemblies are arranged according to the specific pattern the power plant uses. The fuel

Uranium fuel pellets ready
to be placed in fuel rods

assembly depends on the size and generating capacity of the reactor where it will be used. Once the fuel rods are assembled, they can then be shipped to nuclear power plants.

CREATING AND CONTROLLING FISSION

A nuclear reactor is the heart of a nuclear plant, where the fission process can be controlled in order to produce heat. The heat generated by fission is then transmitted to water, which is heated to boiling until it creates steam. The process takes place in a continuous loop, generating more heat and more steam. This steam then turns the blades of huge turbines, which produce electricity. The electricity produced eventually is routed to homes and businesses, where we use it to power everything from air conditioners to cell phone chargers.

FISSION V. FUSION

Nuclear fusion is a term that sounds much like *nuclear fission* but means the opposite. Nuclear fission is the release of energy when atoms split apart. Nuclear fusion also releases energy but does so when two atoms combine. Fusion happens when two nuclei join together to make a larger nucleus. The most familiar example of nuclear fusion is the sun: it fuses hydrogen atoms into helium atoms through nuclear fusion, which then gives off large amounts of heat, light, and radiation.

The fission process must be carefully controlled because of the huge amount of power it creates. Uncontrolled fission, the source of power in an atomic bomb, can lead to explosions and leaked radioactive materials.

Fission is controlled using a series of control rods made of chemical elements that absorb neutrons. These are inserted and withdrawn into the uranium fuel assemblies that create the fission process inside the reactor. The control rods, when inserted, absorb the neutrons and slow or even stop the fission process's chain reaction. A control rod acts like a car's brake when it is inserted and like an accelerator when it is withdrawn.

The power of nuclear fission applies a lot of stress to fuel rods. Advances are being made in fuel rod technology to prevent damage and accidents. In 2011, the Tennessee Valley Authority employees at the Browns Ferry nuclear energy facility in Alabama received an award for developing a method, called XEDOR, which uses real-time stress monitoring to prevent defects that could release radiation from pellets in fuel rods.

Nuclear fission research continues to create nuclear power safely and efficiently. Design, construction, and operation of nuclear power plants and reactors also play an important role in controlling and creating nuclear power.

CHAPTER 5

NUCLEAR PLANTS AND REACTORS

All nuclear power plants share basic features. Each has a containment building to enclose the nuclear reactor, a reactor core where nuclear energy is converted to thermal energy, a turbine building where the thermal energy is converted into electricity, and facilities for storing spent fuel.

The nuclear reactor core is the heart of the nuclear power plant and is not visible from outside the building. The nuclear reactor is housed within a protective structure called the reactor vessel, which is in turn located inside the containment building. All power plant buildings are made of concrete reinforced with steel. The NRC requires a plant to be built to withstand any natural disasters possible in its location, including earthquakes, fires, floods, and tornadoes.

« **Cooling towers are typically hourglass shaped and are the most recognized part of a nuclear power plant.**

PWR AND BWR

All nuclear power plants in the United States are one of two types: the Pressurized Water Reactor (PWR) and the Boiling Water Reactor (BWR). Both of these types are categorized as Light Water Reactors (LWR), which are very similar to conventional power plants except they use nuclear fuel, rather than coal or oil, to generate the heat that turns water to steam.

While both plants are classified under LWRs, each plant operates in a slightly different way. A PWR keeps the water in its system under pressure but does not heat it to the point of boiling. In a PWR, there are two loops to take the heat generated by the nuclear reaction and turn it into steam to run the turbines that generate electricity. One loop carries water through the nuclear core itself and then through a heat exchanger (which creates steam) and then back into the core. This is a closed loop, and the water that touches the reactor never leaves the loop. A second closed loop carries water that is pumped through the other side of the heat exchanger, where it

COOLING SYSTEMS

A nuclear reactor needs to have a system for cooling, both to keep the reactor from overheating and to condense steam. The cooling towers on the plant are often the traditional hourglass-shaped structures that many people identify with a nuclear plant, but some plants use banks of fans in a lower structure to cool plant water. The cooling system allows the reuse of steam produced by cooling it back into water, which can then be reheated and reused in the reaction process. The system that condenses steam back into water—which never comes into direct contact with water that has been exposed to the radioactive materials inside the reactor—usually comes from a nearby source such as a river, lake, or ocean. This is why nuclear power plants are often built in coastal areas or along rivers. Once the cooling water absorbs the heat from the steam, turning the steam back to water, it is usually piped into a cooling tower where its temperature will drop as it releases harmless heat into the atmosphere. Once it has cooled, this circulating water will be reused in the system again as cooling water.

picks up the heat from the first loop, and flows to a generator where the steam turns a turbine, creating electricity. The electricity generated is then carried by electric transmission lines to where it can be accessed by utility customers both in businesses and private homes.

The steam gets condensed back into water and carried through the heat exchanger again in another continuous loop. The steam generator essentially "exchanges" the heat from one loop of water to the other. The water from the reactor, which is heated by fission, and the second batch of water, which absorbs the heat from that first batch to become steam and run the turbine, are in separate pipes and never mix.

The BWR also uses water to create steam and generate electricity through turbines. But in a BWR, the water that becomes steam passes directly through the reactor and then directly to the turbine. It is a more direct system than the PWR because the nuclear reaction heats the water directly within the reactor, and the steam created rises to the top of the reactor vessel to be piped to the turbine to create electricity rather than going through an exchanger and transferring heat to another pipe of water first, as in a PWR. The steam is then condensed back into water by a closed loop of cooling water that comes from the cooling towers of the plant. Once condensed, the water can be moved through the reactor and reheated again during nuclear fission.

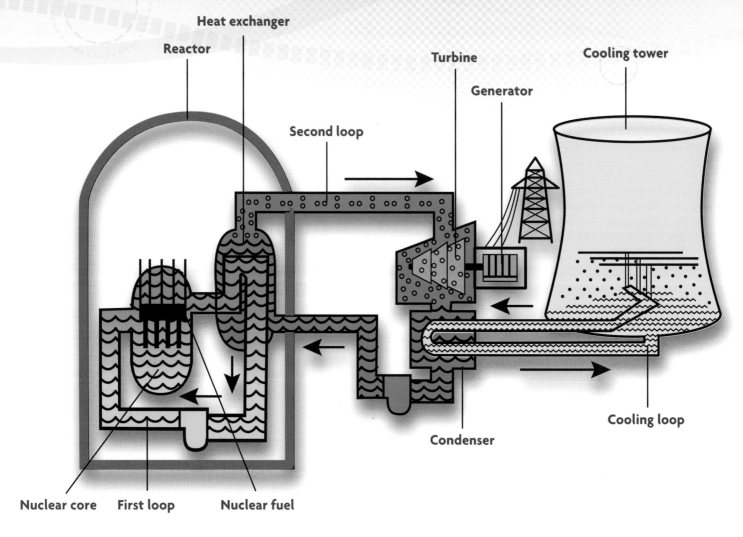

Reactor

Heat exchanger

Turbine

Generator

Cooling tower

Second loop

Nuclear core   First loop   Nuclear fuel

Condenser

Cooling loop

PRESSURIZED WATER REACTOR

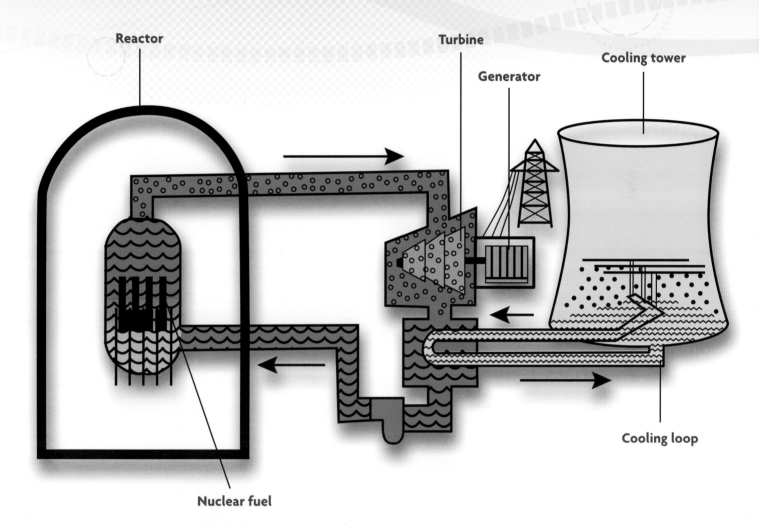

Reactor

Turbine

Generator

Cooling tower

Nuclear fuel

Cooling loop

BOILING WATER REACTOR

The water that runs through the reactor turning to steam and being cooled is constantly reused, never leaving the system and getting used again and again to make electricity.

In addition to energy to create electricity, the fission process also emits radioactivity and creates radioactive waste. Because of this, everything that is exposed to radiation during the fission process in a nuclear plant—the water, fuel rods, reactor, and waste—must be carefully dealt with and contained. Extensive regulations and safety procedures govern the handling of radioactive materials in the industry.

The NRC regulates nuclear power in the United States. It is an organization that enforces safety in all aspects of nuclear power, including granting the license and license renewals all US nuclear power plants need to legally operate. The NRC also oversees waste management practices and operation of processing plants to ensure protocol is followed precisely. In December of 1979, the Institute of Nuclear Power Operations (INPO) was also established, in response to the reports following the Three Mile Island accident. Its purpose was to investigate

BUILDING A NUCLEAR POWER PLANT

Because of all the agencies and regulations involved in the construction of a new nuclear power plant, it is a process that takes a very long time. Before construction can even begin, there is a long and complicated licensing and regulation process, from choosing a site to ensuring that all plans and materials meet the standards and regulations set forth by the NRC and INPO. Plants are inspected at every stage of construction and then again before they begin operation. There is a detailed and involved licensing process before the plant becomes fully functional, as well. Personnel must also be trained and licensed. It can take 7 to 12 years to build a plant and reach the point where it generates electricity.[1] Advocates of nuclear power have pointed out that, as the nation's existing nuclear plants are aging and nearing the end of their life cycle, it is very important that construction begins on new plants as soon as possible.

what had taken place and what changes to the industry might be needed. The INPO's mission is "to promote the highest levels of safety and reliability – to promote excellence – in the operation of commercial nuclear power plants."[2] The INPO's duties include evaluating nuclear plants for safety and reliability, training and accrediting personnel and plants, analyzing events that take place and exchanging information about them, and helping nuclear plants with any technical or management issues they might encounter.

THE NEXT GENERATION?

Reactor designers continue to research and work on smaller, safer designs for nuclear reactors. South Africa began experimenting with pebble-bed reactors in the 1990s that used enriched uranium dioxide encased in billiard ball–sized graphite pebbles. These pebbles would not become hot enough to melt, preventing the type of fuel meltdown many people fear with conventional nuclear plants. However, funding for research and development of the project ended in 2010.

Another project exploring uses of nuclear power is the Next Generation Nuclear Plant (NGNP), which is a project of the Idaho National Laboratory. Its goal is to design new types of nuclear power plants that will be safer and create more effective ways of producing power. The NGNP is based on the use of a High Temperature Gas Reactor. According to a report by

At a nuclear power plant, workers are dressed in full radiation hazmat protection suits: multilayered suits made of cotton, Tyvek, which is a dense synthetic material, and other impenetrable materials. In extremely radioactive areas, some are also wearing respirators and goggles. These workers are inside the containment building of a nuclear power plant, getting ready to remove spent nuclear fuel from the reactor itself and move it to a spent fuel pool where it will be stored. The workers need to carefully follow protocol to avoid accidents.

Huge bolts are undone and the heavy stainless steel dome covering the reactor vessel is removed. A crane moves the heavy dome to one side. The suited workers stand on the refueling bridge above the reactor. They use a grappling device to reach remotely into the reactor where scorching-hot nuclear fission has created radioactive waste and latch on to a nuclear fuel assembly, which contains that radioactive waste. Another worker stands nearby with a set of binoculars to guide the operator of the grappling clamp as he finds, clamps onto, and removes a fuel assembly, which is underwater. If the operator makes even a slight misstep, small amounts of radioactive gas could be leaked into the water. The fuel assembly is slowly lifted, but kept underwater to prevent radiation from entering the atmosphere. Once the fuel assembly is clear of the reactor, it is carefully moved sideways to a small, watery channel called the cattle chute. The operator moves the assembly through the cattle chute into the spent fuel pool, where it will be delicately lowered into a designated slot, still underwater. The operators must keep

Nuclear power plant workers in Brazil monitor contamination levels during a January 2006 refueling.

careful track of where the fuel assemblies go. The assemblies removed from the center of the reactor have burned most thoroughly and are left in the spent fuel pool to cool and remained contained. The assemblies from the outside of the reactor are shuffled inward because they are still useful as fuel. The entire process is regulated and must be observed and documented by trained staff. This process is called refueling, and it takes place in a nuclear power plant every 18 months to two years.

An employee works at the Idaho National Laboratory, where the Next Generation Nuclear Plant is being developed.

the NGNP deputy project director, the innovative reactor provides more industrial options than current technology, which operates at approximately 572 degrees Fahrenheit (300°C).[3] The report states, "The high temperature gas-cooled reactor can provide heat for industrial process[es] at temperatures from 700 to 950°C [1300 to 1750 degrees Fahrenheit]."[4] It uses a small fuel particle with a kernel of enriched uranium embedded in layers of carbon and silicon.

This project is especially interesting for the future, as it would create links between certain industries, such as fertilizers, plastics, and gas refining. These industries could use the residual steam heat left from the fission process and electric generation to fuel some of their industrial applications. This nuclear energy could be used to melt plastics at the high temperatures needed to reuse existing recycled plastic. It could also increase production in oil refineries, as well as reduce the need for fossil fuels that produce carbon emissions. The NGNP would be a partnership between the overall production of electricity and the residual energy that could be used for these industrial purposes.

Although many innovations improving efficiency and safety are in the works, radioactive waste—or radwaste, as it is called within the nuclear industry—is an unavoidable part of the nuclear fission process. After generation, the radioactive waste created from nuclear fission must be stored, either within the plant itself, or transported to another storage facility. Figuring out what to do with radioactive waste is one of the biggest issues surrounding nuclear power and its future.

CHAPTER 6

NUCLEAR WASTE

There are different types of radioactive waste that vary according to how radioactive they are. Each must be handled and disposed of in a different way.

Low-level radioactive waste includes items that have become contaminated with radiation by coming into direct contact with radioactive material. This kind of waste is not just generated by nuclear power plants, but also from hospitals and laboratories in cleaning supplies, medical equipment, and even laboratory animal carcasses or tissues. Low-level waste can also include materials that are more highly radioactive, such as discarded parts from inside a nuclear power plant's reactor vessel. Low-level waste is classified by variations of how radioactive it is. If it is too radioactive, it is no longer classified as low-level waste.

« All nuclear waste must be disposed of carefully, even low level. Crates and casks of waste sit at the Barnwell, South Carolina, low-level disposal site.

At a nuclear power plant, low-level waste is generally stored onsite, where it decays until it can be disposed of as regular trash or until enough accumulates so that it can be shipped to a special low-level waste disposal site. According to the NRC, the disposal site's operator must have a plan of how the facility will function in thousands of years, as radiation will still be present in some waste.

High-level radioactive waste consists of waste that is generated within the actual nuclear reactor, making it much more radioactive than lower-level wastes. High-level waste includes used reactor fuel, called spent fuel, or the waste products left over after spent fuel is reprocessed, a practice that is not currently practiced within the United States. Spent fuel is so potent that it must be handled with extreme care, with enough shielding—20 feet (6 m) of water or a thick metal or concrete canister filled with inert gas—to protect the health of nuclear plant workers and the general public.[1] Because spent fuel

US LOW-LEVEL WASTE SITES

As of 2012, there are three low-level waste disposal sites in the United States: one in Barnwell, South Carolina; one in Clive, Utah; and one in Richland, Washington. According to the NRC Web site, an oversight program enacts periodic inspections at each facility to ensure incoming disposals are properly analyzed and documented, and safety disposal requirements are met.

Spent fuel (high-level waste) stored in deep water at Progress Energy's Shearon Harris nuclear plant in New Hill, North Carolina

can remain dangerous for thousands of years, it must be handled and stored in a way that will protect the public for a very long time.

Currently, used fuel rods are often stored in pools of water within the nuclear plant itself. Radiation does not travel well through water, which makes it a good shield. These pools are called spent-fuel pools, and the water is deep enough to provide a shielding layer of approximately 40 feet (12 m) of water, deep enough that workers can actually walk around the top of the open pool without being exposed to dangerous levels of radiation. The pools are constructed to withstand even earthquakes and are lined with stainless steel to prevent leakage. Spent fuel must stay in the pool for at least one year before it decays enough to be removed to a different type of storage, such as dry cask storage or storage at a specially constructed facility. As of 2011, there are even seven decommissioned nuclear power plants, which are plants that no longer generate electricity, that still have spent fuel stored in pools within their facilities. Some spent fuel is now stored in dry casks, or concrete casks, on the nuclear plant site as spent fuel pools start to fill up. The NRC describes these casks as "typically steel cylinders that are either welded or bolted closed. The steel cylinder provides containment of the spent fuel. Each cylinder is surrounded by additional steel, concrete, or other material to provide radiation shielding to workers and members of the public."[2] Once in the casks, spent fuel remains there until it can be removed once a permanent disposal is in place.

YUCCA MOUNTAIN

Because nuclear power plants have a finite amount of space for storing radioactive waste, the government's goal is to create a permanent storage facility where nuclear waste from all US plants could be stored. Utilities with nuclear power plants are required to contribute money into a fund for the purpose of constructing a site like this. This kind of storage facility would be located underground in geologic spaces mined into mountains or deep below the earth's surface. These sites would have multiple barriers in place to keep the radioactive waste from leaking. Waste generated by reprocessing used fuel can be mixed with glass and immobilized until it becomes something known as vitrified waste, which is then placed in canisters. Spent fuel would be sealed inside containers of stainless steel or copper, which resist corrosion. The containers are designed for indefinite storage of the nuclear waste.

In 1987, Congress passed an amendment naming Yucca Mountain in Nevada as its chosen site for a permanent waste storage facility. A few years later, as research and planning were

WASTE CONFIDENCE DECISION

In 1984, the NRC adopted the Waste Confidence Decision, which was intended to assess the feasibility of creating an offsite storage facility for spent nuclear fuel. If that was not possible, the decision ensured that there would be sufficient onsite storage for the fuel at plants themselves. The decision was updated in 1990, 1999 and 2010. In its 2010 update, the decision ruled that it was technically feasible to create a long-term storage site, at least one repository will be available by the time nuclear plants have exceeded their onsite storage capacity, and that spent fuel can be safely stored onsite for at least 60 years past the license expiration of that particular plant, which is twice as long as plants were originally allowed to store waste once they had been decommissioned. The decision is meant to reassure the nuclear industry that the NRC will continue to provide the industry with options for waste disposal and storage.

underway, the Energy Policy Act of 1992 required that the EPA create specific standards for protecting the public and environment living near Yucca Mountain. Over the next two decades, an enormous amount of time and money was devoted to the research, preparation of the complex license application, and actual development of the project in order to comply with regulations. These regulations included protecting the public from exposure for more than 10,000 years. In 2005, the EPA altered the exposure standard. For the first 10,000 years, the population was not to be exposed to more than 15 millirems (0.15 mSv) per year. The ruling extended the protection period through 1 million years. But with the time extension, the amount of emitted radiation allowed was also raised: for the years after 10,000 and up to 1 million, the amount of emitted radiation was not to exceed 350 millirems (3.5 mSv) per year.[3]

In addition to time and budget troubles, other concerns arose. The Nuclear Waste Policy Act placed a capacity for storage at Yucca Mountain site at a limit of approximately 77,000 short tons (70,000 metric tons) of waste.[4] According to a Congressional Budget Office testimony in 2007, the DOE estimated approximately 72,000 short tons (65,000 metric tons) were slated to be disposed of at Yucca Mountain.[5] The DOE also estimated that US nuclear power plants created approximately 2,200 short tons (2,000 metric tons) of waste each year, and therefore, the amount of waste generated would exceed Yucca Mountain's capacity even before it was scheduled to open.[6]

A DOE employee and an Office of Nuclear Safety and Standards employee stand behind the collection of paperwork making up the Yucca Mountain application in June 2008.

Almost immediately after the site was chosen, politicians from Nevada were lobbying to close down the Yucca Mountain site. In 2010, President Barack Obama put a stop to the project and appointed a committee to explore other disposal options. In March of 2010, the DOE attempted to withdraw its application to construct the repository at Yucca Mountain. A few months later, in June, the NRC ruled that the DOE could not withdraw the application. However, by October of 2010, work on the Yucca Mountain facility had stopped. As of 2012, Yucca Mountain's future is still undetermined, as the administration of President Obama has terminated the project. The DOE is seeking alternative solutions.

Experts in the nuclear industry fear the government's inability to solve the problem of long-term radioactive waste disposal will negatively affect the future of nuclear energy in the United States. It is possible that the immediate solution would be a combination of dry-cask storage at nuclear plant sites and building several intermediate storage facilities in different parts of the country. There is widespread belief it may also be wise to design these sites to be temporary and allow retrieval of spent fuel. The main reason to make the intermediate storage facilities retrievable is because the spent fuel will ultimately need to be put in a geologic repository. There are currently no geologic repositories, however, and so spent fuel is now being stored in intermediate sites for decades.

« **Decisions deeming Yucca Mountain a nuclear waste site and then motions to shut it down have created political debate for many years.**

NUCLEAR WASTE INNOVATIONS

New technologies for cleaning up nuclear waste are being developed, particularly that which might be left after an accident or spill. A blue goo called DeconGel, developed by CBI Polymers Inc, can be painted or sprayed on surfaces contaminated by radiation. Once the goo dries, it peels up, taking the radioactive contamination with it. The leftover layer is considered low-level waste and must be disposed of accordingly. The company donated 500 gallons (1,900 L) of DeconGel to aid in cleanup efforts following the 2011 disaster in Japan, which were poured on everything from school playgrounds to parking lots and retail stores.

Another innovation in accident cleanup focuses on an isotope called Strontium-90. Strontium-90 is a radioactive material produced during nuclear fission that remains contained in spent nuclear fuel. Researchers from Northwestern University and the Argonne National Laboratory are working on a way to use freshwater pond algae to remove the Strontium-90 from liquid nuclear waste so that it would not contaminate anything with radiation in the event of an accident. The algae has the natural ability to soak up and sequester different biominerals, including natural strontium, which is not radioactive. Researchers are looking into whether the algae could do the same thing with the radioactive Strontium-90.[7]

Innovations called fast reactors aim to reduce the amount of waste created in the first place. Several prototypes have been built in the United States, France, Japan and Russia. The Toshiba 4S (Super Safe, Small, and Simple) is one such reactor and is designed to use liquid sodium as a coolant, which allows it to run hotter than if water were used as a coolant. This would mean less nuclear fission needed to produce the same amount of power, and therefore less radioactive waste produced. The Power Reactor Innovative Small Modular (PRISM) being developed by Hitachi and General Electric is another small sodium-cooled reactor, but it is powered by the used nuclear fuel from traditional water-cooled reactors, which would also alleviate concerns over radioactive waste produced. The remaining challenge to fast reactors concern reconciling economics and policy of using the devices.

SPENT FUEL IN THE UNITED STATES

According to the Congressional Research Service estimates using NEI data, approximately 78 percent of the more than 68,000 short tons (60,000 metric tons) of commercial spent fuel in the Unites States in 2009 were in pools. The other approximate 22 percent were in dry casks.[8] Most nuclear waste—approximately 97 percent—can be recycled and reprocessed and used again.[9] However, this is not currently practiced in the United States. If it was, the spent fuel could potentially run the reactors in the United States for approximately 30 years before requiring any new uranium, according to the World Nuclear Association in 2012.[10]

A Toshiba employee with the miniature Toshiba 4S reactor, which the company claims will not need to be refueled for approximately 30 years

Scientists are also working on fission-fusion hybrid reactors that could destroy components of nuclear waste bred by the creation of nuclear power. These systems could also be configured to breed new nuclear fuel from the waste. Some waste generated through fission can be reprocessed, but there is also some leftover, long-lived waste that cannot be reused. Fusion can be used to burn this waste. In a University of Texas at Austin article in 2009, a group of plasma scientists discussed an innovation called a Compact Fusion Neutron Source (CFNS). The device would have a plasma core where fusion would be used to create neutrons. These neutrons would incite fission in a surrounding blanket of fissile material that could include nuclear waste. The CFNS's burning of long-lived waste would create energy, and the device would be compact. According to the university's article, "One hybrid would be needed to destroy the waste produced by 10 to 15 LWRs [light water reactors]."[11]

The many innovations in waste management and efficient nuclear energy creation aim to resolve many issues surrounding radioactive nuclear waste. Continued research addressing radiation and waste will be significant to the future of nuclear power, as will taking a close look at the many advantages of this type of energy.

CHAPTER 7

THE BENEFITS OF NUCLEAR POWER

Many people believe nuclear power's potential should be expanded. According to a *Wall Street Journal* writer,

The argument for nuclear power can be stated pretty simply: We have no choice. If the world intends to address the threat of global warming and still satisfy its growing appetite for electricity, it needs an ambitious expansion of nuclear power.[1]

MORE POWER

One of the biggest advantages of nuclear energy is that it can produce a lot of energy from a small amount of fuel. The energy density created from uranium nuclear fission is substantially greater than from fossil fuels. Two pounds (1 kg) of oil generate approximately four kilowatt hours. One kilowatt hour is a unit of energy equal to

« **Compared to both fossil fuels and alternative energy sources such as wind power, nuclear energy is much more powerful.**

1,000 watts, which is the wattage of some hair dryers. A 1,000 watt hair dryer running for one hour of time uses one kilowatt hour of energy.[2] Two pounds (1 kg) of uranium fuel generate 400,000 kilowatt hours of electricity.[3] In physical terms, "a pound of uranium is smaller than a baseball and is roughly equivalent to a million gallons of gasoline, which would fill a cube. . . as tall as a five-story building," according to the DOE Web site.[4]

Nuclear energy has another power advantage as well: reliable base-load power. Base-load power refers to the constant demand for energy around the clock, or 24 hours a day. Nuclear power is one of the best sources of base-load power because nuclear plants are designed to run at full power for months at a time. Other alternative energies, including solar, wind, and water power, on the other hand, are intermittent sources because they are dependent on changing, unpredictable conditions.

BULK OF CLEAN US ENERGY

As of 2012, approximately 30 percent of energy used in the United States was emissions-free, meaning the energy source does not produce carbon emissions. Nuclear energy accounted for the bulk of that number, supplying approximately 70 percent of all carbon-free electricity.[5]

LESS POLLUTION

Compared to fossil fuels, nuclear fission produces fewer emissions of carbon dioxide, nitrogen oxides, and sulfur dioxides, all of which can be harmful to the environment and humans. Opponents argue, however, that while nuclear power may be cleaner for the environment when it actually generates power, it is not as clean before and after the fission process. Before, uranium must be mined, which requires equipment that produces greenhouse gases. Energy sources such as solar and wind power are often praised for being green choices with minimal environmental damage in their implementation. Supporters of nuclear energy claim that although the mining process may not be completely green, its carbon footprint is minimal. States a *Wall Street Journal* article, "Even when taking into account 'full life-cycle emissions'— including mining of uranium, shipping fuel, constructing plants and managing waste—nuclear's carbon-dioxide discharges are . . . less than solar power."[6]

"Nuclear energy is simply the only nonpolluting energy source that can replace fossil fuels. It's a fairy tale that wind and solar can do the job."[7]**—Patrick Moore, cochair of Clean and Safe Energy Coalition (CASEnergy) and cofounder of Greenpeace**

These small uranium pellets provide many times more power than fossil fuels relative to their size, and the leftover waste is smaller than the pellet itself.

LESS WASTE

Nuclear energy generates less waste than fossil fuels relative to the amount of energy it provides. Advocates of nuclear power claim that if a family of four used nuclear energy over its

entire lifetimes, the amount of vitrified waste generated would only be the size of a golf ball.[8]
Using one barrel of oil provides approximately 19 gallons (72 l) of gasoline, which is more than
one tank of gas in an average car.[9] It also creates more than 947 pounds (430 kg)—of carbon
dioxide.[10] In comparison to the amount of toxic waste produced by other industries, including
fossil fuel energy generation, radioactive waste makes up only 0.001 percent of the total amount
of hazardous industrial waste as of 2012.[11] According to the NEI,

> *Over the past four decades, the entire industry has produced about 67,500 metric tons*
> *[74,400 short tons] of used nuclear fuel. If used fuel assemblies were stacked end-to-*
> *end and side-by-side, this would cover a football field about seven yards deep.[12]*

The nuclear industry is also the only one that adds the cost of dealing with waste into the
cost of its product. Disposing of and storing nuclear fission byproduct is carefully regulated.
Some even claim that what is leftover from the fission process should not be considered waste
because it can be repurposed. Although not practiced in the United States, a large portion
of radioactive spent fuel can be reprocessed and reused again in fission. As for the lesser
amount of spent fuel that is not repurposed, although it is radioactive, it gradually becomes less
hazardous over time.

Plateau Resources, Ltd.

SHOOTARING MILL

2 MILES

Please Don't Litter

« Presidents of a Utah uranium milling company near the sign to their domestic operation

DOMESTIC SOURCE, LESS LAND

In the United States, it is possible to complete all steps in nuclear power creation domestically. These include mining the uranium used for fuel, creating nuclear fission at a power plant, and transmitting the electricity produced. Although much of the uranium used in the United States today is imported, the uranium production industry is looking into increasing domestic supplies.

This would provide a more independent and secure form of power than other energy sources, such as fossil fuels. Many estimate there to be large deposits of uranium in the United States that have not yet been discovered or mined. For example, it was estimated that an undeveloped uranium deposit in the community of Coles Hill, Virginia, held 119 million pounds (53 million kg). It was also estimated this was enough uranium to fuel the entire state's nuclear reactors for 75 years.[13]

Of the domestic land used to create the energy, nuclear power plants are an efficient use of land. It would take 60 square miles (155 sq km) of solar panels or anywhere from 15 to 180 square miles (39 to 140 sq km) of wind turbines to produce the same amount of electricity as a single nuclear power plant in a confined location.[14] Nuclear power plants typically take up less than one square mile (2.5 sq km).

SAFETY STANDARDS

Perhaps the strongest arguments against nuclear power, and the ones that have most swayed public opinion, refer to accidents that have taken place since the boom years of nuclear plant

"The discovery of nuclear chain reactions need not bring about the destruction of mankind any more than did the discovery of matches. We only must do everything in our power to safeguard against its abuse."[15]—**Albert Einstein**

construction. These accidents have prompted new levels of regulation for nuclear power. There are two regulatory organizations within the nuclear power industry: the NRC issues licenses and ensures proper procedures are strictly adhered to, and the EPA regulates nuclear waste. Following the regulations set forth by these organizations is required in the implementation of any nuclear energy project, and the organizations receive continual government and public scrutiny to ensure standards are as thorough as possible. Additionally, while these are the only organizations that regulate the US nuclear power industry, several organizations exist to inform, support, or oversee nuclear power production as well. One such organization is the US DOE, whose Office of Nuclear Energy focuses on advancing nuclear power to meet the needs of the United States. Additional functions of the Office of Nuclear Energy include supporting both peaceful and safe uses of nuclear energy, as well as overseeing the front-end of the process, such as the mining and processing of uranium ore. As consideration of increased nuclear power use continues, safety and standards are sure to remain at the forefront of discussion.

« **Steven Chu, the US Secretary of Energy in 2012, worked for a US energy agenda to decrease dependence on fossil fuels.**

CHAPTER  8

A FRESH LOOK

As innovations providing solutions to nuclear energy's disadvantages are developed and the need to reduce or eliminate fossil fuel dependencies becomes more urgent, it is undeniable the world's future energy practices will undergo change. Alternative energies that are sustainable, renewable, and greener than fossil fuels will continue to be researched, improved, and implemented.

As is the case with other energy sources, alternative energies, including nuclear power, are not a perfect solution. Although it can be generated without reliance on foreign sources, nuclear power is hampered by the prohibitively high cost of researching and building new reactors, both traditional reactors and newer experimental types. The nuclear power industry is also faced with finding solutions and developing methods for limiting and storing radioactive waste, and overcoming fear

« **Many researchers and developers are giving nuclear energy and other alternative energies significant consideration for the future.**

and scrutiny from past accidents. However, despite these complexities, the threat of climate change and the need to lower carbon emissions are significant issues that nuclear power could help alleviate. According to a comprehensive study of nuclear energy by the Massachusetts Institute of Technology (MIT),

> The nuclear option should be retained precisely because it is an important carbon-free source of power. . . . Taking nuclear power off the table as a viable alternative will prevent the global community from achieving long-term gains in the control of carbon dioxide emissions.[1]

THE KYOTO PROTOCOL

Many countries have already committed to alternatives to fossil fuels, including increased nuclear energy. On February 16, 2005, in the city of Kyoto, Japan, countries attending the United Nations Framework Convention on Climate Change signed a treaty with the specific goal of reducing greenhouse gas emissions. The Kyoto Protocol is a legally binding agreement which the countries that ratified it made to lower their greenhouse gas emissions by at least 5 percent from 1990 levels, calculated as an average from 2008 to 2012. This represents an approximate 29 percent cut compared to emissions expected without the Kyoto Protocol.[2] The Kyoto Protocol was an important step in making nuclear energy a more attractive method for

Minister Wangari Maathai of Kenya on February 16, 2005, at the Commemorative Event to Mark the Entry into Force of the Kyoto Protocol

producing electricity because it is an energy source that does not create greenhouse gases. More than 190 countries ratified the treaty as of August 2012, but the United States had not. For the countries that did ratify the treaty to reduce greenhouse emissions, nuclear energy was a viable way to meet their obligations while providing their countries with sufficient power.

One idea for a new nuclear technology that could benefit countries everywhere is the use of reactors built into ships, which could travel to where energy is needed. One such ship was in development and undergoing safety testing in Russia in 2011, with several more planned for future development in the country. However, there is also some debate and concern over the safety and stability of floating nuclear power plants, especially in regard to withstanding hurricanes and tsunamis.

There are also plans for nuclear reactors that are sealed for life, with the fuel inside, which would last 30 years and then be disposed of without refueling and the risks associated with it.

WILL NUCLEAR ENERGY BECOME RENEWABLE?

Is nuclear energy a renewable source of power? Not at the moment. Biofuels such as ethanol or biodiesel are renewable because they come from plants and can be replenished by growing more plants. Solar power is also considered renewable, as the sun shines on most days and returns after cloudy days. Wind power is also renewable, as wind blows naturally and continually in various locations around the globe. Nuclear energy requires using uranium, of which there is a finite amount on earth. Once that fuel is spent, it must be recycled and reprocessed in order to be used again, a process that is not currently practiced in the United States. Ultimately, the future development of reactors that reuse spent fuel would bring nuclear energy closer to becoming a renewable energy source.

The TerraPower TP-1 is one design of a sealed reactor. The TerraPower TP-1 is filled with U-238 and a smaller amount of enriched uranium within is designed to act as an igniter to incite nuclear fission for several decades. Additional fuel would not have to be added to keep the reaction going, but it could be stopped using control rods if needed. The reaction begins once control rods are removed. Once all the fuel is spent, the waste would remain inside the sealed reactor. However, this innovation is still undergoing testing and also requires uranium that is enriched to more than twice the average today, which would create additional radioactive waste. The TerraPower TP-1 began development in 2006. The company hoped to have a working test model by 2020 and a commercial-ready model later that decade.

THORIUM

New technologies are being developed for nuclear fuel as well. One of these is the possibility of using thorium, a natural, radioactive metal found in most rocks and soil. Thorium research began in the 1950s, but died out in the 1970s for various reasons, including decreased energy demand growth. However, interest in thorium has risen, especially considering its waste properties. Like uranium, thorium is radioactive, but its waste remains so for approximately 500 years, rather than thousands. Still, 500 years is a long time to deal with hazardous waste.

However, scientists have recently discovered that specially created thorium grains can be used to soak up radiation. The grains have tiny pores that soak up harmful positive ions from larger amounts of liquid waste, which means thorium could help remove radiation from existing radiation-contaminated liquids.

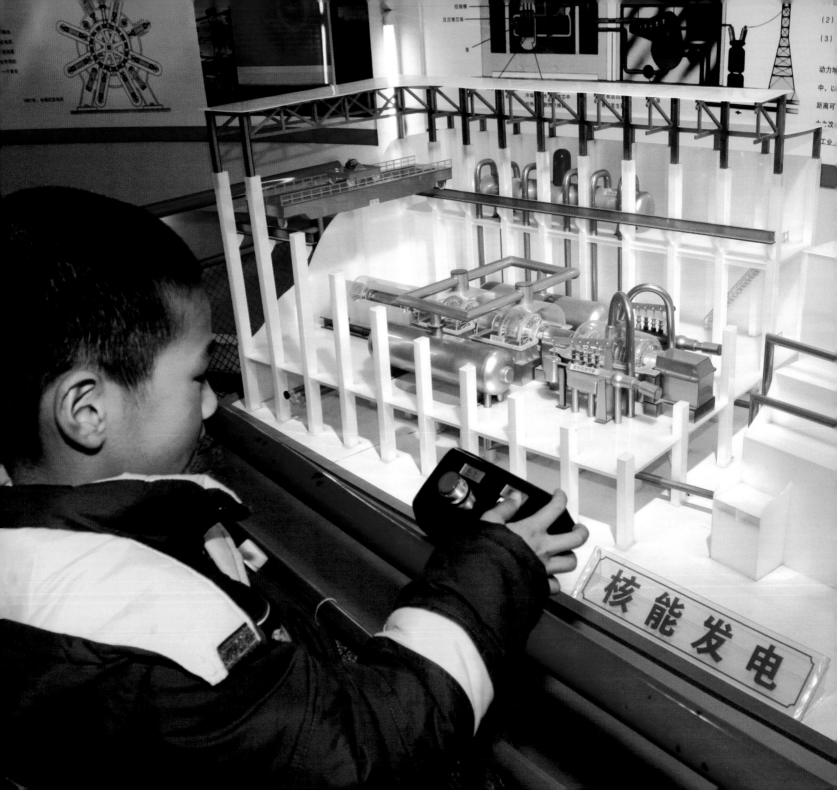

核能发电

INCREASING NUCLEAR KNOWLEDGE

Many organizations exist to promote increased knowledge for the future of the nuclear power industry. One organization, the World Nuclear University, is dedicated to the training of current and prospective employees in the nuclear industry. It holds classes around the world in nuclear power, organization, and leadership, and is dedicated to the peaceful applications of nuclear science and technology. It also holds a Nuclear Energy Olympiad where college students can compete to research and develop a plan for gaining public acceptance of nuclear energy in their country.

The DOE's Office of Nuclear Energy works to expand knowledge and research as well. It has programs that include using supercomputers to simulate new nuclear energy technologies, managing the facilities at the Idaho National Laboratory's nuclear research facilities, working to solve the issues surrounding the safe disposal of nuclear materials, and working to expand the useful lifetimes of existing nuclear plants.

NUCLEAR LEADERS

By 2035, the IAEA projects that China will use 70 percent more energy than the United States. It also forecasts that China, Korea, and India will lead the world in the use of nuclear power to generate energy, with nuclear generation growing by as much as 70 percent in those countries.[3]

A child tests out a nuclear power simulator at the Wuhan Science and Technology Museum in China.

On March 22, 2012, the White House announced the funding of $450 million to develop American-made small modular reactors (SMRs).[4] The reactors would be smaller than average reactors, expecting them to be more manageable and safe, and also more economical. The project aimed to provide licensing for up to two different SMR designs, with the DOE soliciting proposals for projects it felt had promise of being cleared by the Nuclear Regulatory Commission. Then in May of that year, the Office of Energy announced it would fund research on new fuels for LWRs. The goals were to discover "innovative attributes such as higher temperature and strength capability, lower fuel operating temperature and increased resistance to oxidation – all of which could make future reactors even more resistant to accidents," according to the Office of Nuclear Energy Web site.[5]

"Nuclear power may eventually serve as a bridging technology to a fully renewable energy future. Alternatively, nuclear power may experience widespread deployment in many countries over many centuries, as long as humanity remains vigilant in ensuring safe and secure use of peaceful nuclear energy."[6]—**Charles D. Ferguson, *Nuclear Energy: What Everyone Needs to Know***

Building on President Obama's efforts to make college education affordable in the United States, the DOE also announced that May that it would fund "more than $47 million in scholarships, fellowships, research grants, and university research reactor upgrades to train and educate the next generation of leaders in America's nuclear industry."[7]

LOOKING FOR APPROVAL

The future of nuclear energy also depends largely on public opinion. Decisions to construct a new nuclear power plant often depend on long approval processes, as well as the availability of funding for loans to cover the high costs of construction. In 2005, the government announced guaranteed loans for the construction of new reactors as part of the 2005 Energy Policy Act. Public opinion on nuclear power had risen by June of 2010. Many Americans, in the wake of rising energy costs and future energy security, supported the construction of new nuclear power plants. In a CBS News poll taken after the Fukushima nuclear crisis in Japan in 2011, 50 percent of people disapproved of building more US nuclear power plants, which was a 16-point increase since the question was last asked in 2008.[8]

According to the poll, the number of people who supported the construction of new nuclear power plants had fallen to 43 percent.[9] This was even lower than public opinion following the Three Mile Island accident in 1979.

Most experts agree that despite public opinion and the complex history, myths, and policies that surround nuclear energy, it will be an important part of the world's energy future. The power of nuclear energy is clear. Its main challenges are being addressed with viable solutions and alternatives, and new technologies are continually being developed. As researchers and developers continue their work to create safer and more innovative ways to produce nuclear energy, it shows great promise as part of a cleaner energy future.

« Although it is likely nuclear energy will play a role in future energy solutions, public opinion will largely shape the way it is implemented.

GLOSSARY

ATOM—The smallest part of an element that still retains the characteristics of that element.

ATOMIC BOMB—A bomb whose power comes from a fission chain reaction.

CONTAINMENT BUILDING—The structure enclosing the reactor vessel and nuclear fuel at a nuclear power plant, designed to contain anything that might accidentally escape.

CONTROL ROD—A device used to control nuclear fission by regulating the fission process.

CORE—The part of the nuclear reactor that contains nuclear fuel.

ELECTRON—A negatively charged particle that exists outside the nucleus of an atom.

FUEL ROD—A sealed metal tube filled with fuel pellets made usually of uranium.

ISOTOPE—An atom that has a different number of neutrons.

MELTDOWN—When a nuclear reactor core melts due to improper cooling of nuclear fuel.

NEUTRON—A particle with no electric charge, found in the nucleus of an atom, that binds protons together.

NUCLEAR REACTOR—A piece of equipment where a nuclear reaction can be started, maintained and controlled, generating energy.

NUCLEUS—The mass at the center of an atom, consisting of protons and neutrons, which has a positive charge.

PROTON—A positively charged particle in the nucleus of an atom.

RADIATION—Energy emission in the form of particles or waves.

RADIOACTIVITY—Radiation emitted by a nuclear reaction or nuclear decay.

SPENT FUEL POOL—A pool where used nuclear fuel is stored underwater.

TURBINE—A machine that produces power when wind, water, or a gas causes a wheel or rotor to revolve.

URANIUM—An element extracted from certain minerals and used as nuclear fuel.

YELLOWCAKE—Processed uranium ore that is used as the raw material for nuclear fuel.

ADDITIONAL RESOURCES

SELECTED BIBLIOGRAPHY

Atkins, Stephen E. *Historical Encyclopedia of Atomic Energy*. Westport, CT: Greenwood, 2000. Print.

Ferguson, Charles D. *Nuclear Energy: What Everyone Needs to Know*. New York: Oxford UP, 2011. Print.

Hore-Lacy, Ian. *Nuclear Energy in the 21st Century*, 2nd Edition. London: World Nuclear UP, 2011. Print.

Osif, Bonnie A., et al. *TMI 25 Years Later: The Three Mile Island Nuclear Power Plant Accident and Its Impact*. University Park, PA: Pennsylvania State UP, 2006. Print.

FURTHER READINGS

Friedman, Lauri S. *Nuclear Power*. Farmington Hills, MI: Greenhaven, 2009. Print.

Lusted, Marcia Amidon and Greg Lusted. *Building History: A Nuclear Power Plant*. Farmington Hills, MI: Lucent, 2005. Print.

Singer, Neal. *Wonders of Nuclear Fusion: Creating an Ultimate Energy Source*. U of New Mexico P, 2011. Print.

WEB LINKS

To learn more about nuclear energy, visit ABDO Publishing Company online at **www.abdopublishing.com**. Web sites about nuclear energy are featured on our Book Links page. These links are routinely monitored and updated to provide the most current information available.

FOR MORE INFORMATION

For more information on this subject, contact or visit the following organizations:

DEPARTMENT OF ENERGY'S OFFICE OF NUCLEAR ENERGY
1000 Independence Ave. SW, Washington, DC 20585
202-586-5000
http://www.ne.doe.gov

The Office of Nuclear Energy supports and promotes peaceful uses of nuclear energy and research on its development as a resource. Contact the organization for more information on nuclear research being done, new technologies, programs, and advisory committees.

UNITED STATES NUCLEAR REGULATORY COMMISSION
Washington, DC 2055-0001
1-800-368-5642
http://www.nrc.gov

This organization regulates all US nuclear power plants, including operating, licensing, materials, and waste management. Contact the organization to learn more about US nuclear plants.

SOURCE NOTES

CHAPTER 1. NUCLEAR ENERGY AT A GLANCE

1. "World Energy Outlook 2011 Fact Sheet." *International Energy Agency: World Energy Outlook.* International Energy Agency, 2011. Web. 11 Sept. 2012.

2. Yuri Sokolov and Alan McDonald. "Nuclear Power: Global Status and Trends." *International Atomic Energy Agency.* International Atomic Energy Agency, 2006. Web. 11 Sept. 2012.

3. "Power Reactors." *US NRC.* United States Nuclear Regulatory Commission, n.d. Web. 11 Sept. 2012.

4. "Sources of Electricity: United States, 2010." *Vault Electricity.com.* Vault Energy Solutions, 2 Apr. 2011. Web. 11 Sept. 2012.

5. "Benefits of Nuclear Energy." *Idaho National Laboratory.* US Department of Energy, n.d. Web. 11 Sept. 2012.

6. "Nuclear Power's Role in Generating Electricity." *Congressional Budget Office.* n.p., 2 May 2008. Web. 11 Sept. 2012.

7. Bisconti Research. "US Public Opinion about Nuclear Energy Stabilizes." *NEI.* Nuclear Energy Institute, Feb. 2012. Web. 11 Sept. 2012.

CHAPTER 2. THE HISTORY OF NUCLEAR ENERGY

1. "World War II." *Encyclopædia Britannica.* Encyclopædia Britannica, 2012. Web. 11 Sept. 2012.

2. "'Fat Man' Atomic Bomb." *National Museum of the US Air Force.* National Museum of the USAF, 4 Feb. 2011. Web. 11 Sept. 2012.

3. "'Little Boy' Atomic Bomb." *National Museum of the US Air Force.* National Museum of the USAF, 4 Feb. 2011. Web. 11 Sept. 2012.

4. "The Story of Hiroshima." *Hiroshima and Nagasaki Remembered.* AJ Software & Multimedia, n.d. Web. 11 Sept. 2012.

5. "The Atomic Bombings of Hiroshima and Nagasaki : Chapter 10—Total Casualties." *The Avalon Project.* Yale Law School, Lillian Goldman Law Library, 2008. Web. 14 Sept. 2012.

6. "United States Atomic Energy Commission Formed: Part 2." *Y12 National Security Complex.* US Department of Energy, 2012. Web. 11 Sept. 2012.

7. "Atoms for Peace." *IAEA.org.* Vienna International Centre, n.d. Web. 11 Sept. 2012.

8. "Some Important Facts About Nuclear Power." *Nuclear Energy Information Service.* Nuclear Energy Information Service, 2004. Web. 11 Sept. 2012.

9. "Backgrounder on Emergency Preparedness at Nuclear Power Plants." *US NRC.* US Nuclear Regulatory Commission, 4 Feb. 2011. Web. 11 Sept. 2012.

10. Ibid.

11. "Backgrounder on Chernobyl Nuclear Power Plant Accident." *US NRC.* US Nuclear Regulatory Commission, 18 Apr. 2012. Web. 11 Sept. 2012.

12. Ibid.

13. Stephen E. Atkins. *Historical Encyclopedia of Atomic Energy.* Santa Barbara, CA: ABC-CLIO/Greenwood, 2000. Print. 83.

14. "Fukushima Accident 2011." *World Nuclear Association.* World Nuclear Association, 3 Aug. 2012. Web. 11 Sept. 2012.

CHAPTER 3. RADIATION

1. "Deterministic Effects and Stochastic Effects." *Hong Kong Observatory*. RHU Department of Health, 20 Aug. 2012. Web. 11 Sept. 2012.

2. "Radiation Exposure and Cancer." *American Cancer Society: Learn About Cancer*. American Cancer Society, 29 Mar. 2010. Web. 11 Sept. 2012.

3. Bernard L. Cohen. "Risks of Nuclear Power." *ISU Physics*. Idaho State University, n.d. Web. 11 Sept. 2012.

4. "Radiation Exposure and Cancer." *American Cancer Society: Learn About Cancer*. American Cancer Society, 29 Mar. 2010. Web. 11 Sept. 2012.

5. Randall Munroe. "Radiation Dose Chart." *Xkcd.com*. n.p., n.d. Web. 13 Sept. 2012.

6. "Myths & Facts About Radiation." *NEI*. Nuclear Energy Institute, n.d. Web. 11 Sept. 2012.

7. "Daily Doses in Our Lives." *US NRC*. US Nuclear Regulatory Commission, 29 Mar. 2012. Web. 11 Sept. 2012.

8. "Radiation Emergencies: Measuring Radiation." *Centers for Disease Control and Prevention*. USA.gov, n.d. Web. 11 Sept. 2012.

9. EK Pauwels and M. Bourguignon. "Cancer Induction Caused by Radiation Due to Computed Tomography: A Critical Note." *PubMed.gov*. USA.gov, 1 Sept. 2011. Web. 11 Sept. 2012.

10. "Fact Sheet on Biological Effects of Radiation." *US NRC*. US Nuclear Regulatory Commission, 29 Mar. 2012. Web. 11 Sept. 2012.

11. Iain Thomson. "Aussie Scientists Develop Radioactivity-Trapping Nanofibers." *Register*. Register, 3 Nov. 2011. Web. 11 Sept. 2012.

CHAPTER 4. CREATING NUCLEAR ENERGY

1. "History of Nuclear Energy Production." *EBSCO Host Connection*. EBSCO Publishing, n.d. Web. 11 Sept. 2012.

2. "Uranium Quick Facts." *Depleted UF6: Management Information Network*. n.p., n.d. Web. 11 Sept. 2012.

3. Ibid.

4. "What is Uranium? How Does it Work?" *World Nuclear Association*. World Nuclear Association, May 2012. Web. 11 Sept. 2012.

5. "Uranium." *EPA: Radiation Protection*. Environmental Protection Agency, 6 Mar. 2012. Web. 11 Sept. 2012.

CHAPTER 5. NUCLEAR PLANTS AND REACTORS

1. "Some Important Facts About Nuclear Power." *Nuclear Energy Information Service*. Nuclear Energy Information Service, 2004. Web. 13 Sept. 2012.

2. "About Us." *INPO*. Institute of Nuclear Power Operations, n.d. Web. 13 Sept. 2012.

3. Rafael Soto. "Next Generation Nuclear Plant: An Emerging Energy Solution." *PennEnergy*. n. p., n.d. Web. 13 Sept. 2012.

4. Ibid.

CHAPTER 6. NUCLEAR WASTE

1."Spent Fuel Pools." *US NRC*, US Nuclear Regulatory Commission, 29 Mar. 2012. Web. 13 Sept. 2012.

2. "Spent Fuel Storage in Pools and Dry Casks: Key Points and Questions & Answers." *US NRC*. US Nuclear Regulatory Commission, 29 Mar. 2012. Web. 13 Sept. 2012.

3. Environmental Protection Agency. "EPA Yucca Mountain Fact Sheet No. 2." *NuclearFiles.org*. Nuclear Age Peace Foundation, Oct. 2005. Web. 13 Sept. 2012.

4. "Nuclear Waste Management." *GAO*. US Government Accountability Office, Nov. 2009. Web. 13 Sept. 2012.

5. Kim Cawley. "The Federal Government's Liabilities Under the Nuclear Waste Policy Act." Congressional Budget Office. n.p., 4 Oct. 2007. Web. 13 Sept. 2012.

6. Ibid.

7. "Pond Alga Could Help Scientists Design Effective Method for Cleaning Up Nuclear Waste." *Phys.org*. Phys.org, 4 Apr. 2011. Web. 13 Sept. 2011.

8. "Spent Fuel Storage in Pools and Dry Casks: Key Points and Questions & Answers." *US NRC*. US Nuclear Regulatory Commission, 29 Mar. 2012. Web. 13 Sept. 2012.

9. "Waste Management." *World Nuclear Association*. World Nuclear Association, May 2012. Web. 13 Sept. 2012.

10. "Processing of Used Nuclear Fuel." *World Nuclear Association*. World Nuclear Association, May 2012. Web. 13 Sept. 2012.

11. "Nuclear Fusion-Fission Hybrid Could Destroy Nuclear Waste and Contribute to Carbon-Free Energy Future." *University of Texas at Austin*. University of Texas at Austin, 27 Jan. 2009. Web. 13 Sept. 2012.

CHAPTER 7. THE BENEFITS OF NUCLEAR POWER

1. "How to Take a Meter Reading." *Energy Trust of Oregon*. Energy Trust of Oregon, n.d. Web. 13 Sept. 2012.

2. Michael Totty. "The Case For and Against Nuclear Power." *Wall Street Journal*. Dow Jones, 30 June 2008. Web. 13 Sept. 2012.

3. "Nuclear Power Advantages." *ICENS*. International Centre for Environmental and Nuclear Sciences, n.d. Web. 13 Sept. 2012.

4. "All About Nuclear: Making Electricity." *US Department of Energy*. US Department of Energy, n.d. Web. 13 Sept. 2012.

5. "Nuclear Energy Benefits the Environment." *NEI*. Nuclear Energy Institute, n.d. Web. 13 Sept. 2012.

6. Michael Totty. "The Case For and Against Nuclear Power." *Wall Street Journal*. Dow Jones, 30 June 2008. Web. 13 Sept. 2012.

7. Lisa Goff. "Quick Study: The Facts on Nuclear Energy." *Reader's Digest*. Reader's Digest.com, Aug. 2008. Web. 13 Sept. 2012.

8. Bruno Comby. "The Benefits of Nuclear Energy." *EFN*. Environmentalists For Nuclear Energy, n.d. Web. 13 Sept. 2012.

9. "Frequently Asked Questions." *EIA*. US Department of Energy, 5 Sept. 2012. Web. 13 Sept. 2012.

10. Paul Roberts. "The Last Drops: How to Bridge the Gap Between Oil and Green Energy." *PopSci.* Popular Science, 12 Jul. 2011. Web. 13 Sept. 2012.

11. William Barletta, et al. "Clean, Sustainable, Responsible: Nuclear Power for the US." *Laboratory for Nuclear Science.* Massachusetts Institute for Technology, Mar. 2010. Web. 13 Sept. 2012.

12. "Nuclear Waste: Amounts and On-Site Storage." *NEI.* Nuclear Energy Institute, n.d. Web. 13 Sept. 2012.

13. Jessica Sabbath. "General Assembly to Weigh Pros, Cons of Uranium Mining." *Virginia Business.* Virginia Business Publications, 27 Dec. 2011. Web. 13 Sept. 2012.

14. "Benefits of Nuclear Energy." *Idaho National Laboratory.* US Department of Energy, n.d. Web. 13 Sept. 2012.

15. "Quotes of Albert Einstein." Department of Physics and Astronomy. Augustana College, n.d. Web. 13 Sept. 2012.

CHAPTER 8. A FRESH LOOK

1. "The Future of Nuclear Power." *MIT.* Massachusetts Institute of Technology, 2009. Web. 13 Sept. 2012.

2. "Green Ribbon Climate Action Task Force: Kyoto Protocol." *City of Tacoma.* n. p., 2010. Web. 13 Sept. 2012.

3. "World Energy Outlook 2011 Fact Sheet." *International Energy Agency: World Energy Outlook.* International Energy Agency, 2011. Web. 11 Sept. 2012.

4. "Obama Administration Announces $450 Million to Design and Commercialize US Small Modular Nuclear Reactors." *US Department of Energy, News Room.* US Department of Energy, 22 Mar. 2012. Web. 13 Sept. 2012.

5. "Office of Nuclear Energy Announces Funding to Advance Accident Tolerant Nuclear Reactor Fuel." *US Department of Energy, News Room.* US Department of Energy, 2 May 2012. Web. 13 Sept. 2012.

6. Charles D. Ferguson. *Nuclear Energy: What Everyone Needs to Know.* New York: Oxford UP, 2011. *Google Book Search.* Web. 13 Sept. 2012.

7. "Energy Department Announces New Investments to Train Next Generation of Nuclear Energy Leaders, Advance University-Led Nuclear Innovation." *US Department of Energy, News Room.* US Department of Energy, 8 May 2012. Web. 13 Sept. 2012.

8. Brian Montopoli. "Poll: Support for New Nuclear Plants Drops." CBS News. CBS Interactive, 22 Mar. 2011. Web. 13 Sept. 2012.

9. Ibid.

INDEX

accidents, 13, 25–31, 38, 53, 60, 62, 76, 87–89, 92, 98, 99
atomic bomb, 18–19, 53
Atomic Energy Commission, 20, 22, 23, 25

Banana Equivalent Dose, 37
Boiling Water Reactor, 56–57, 59

cancer, 34–37, 41, 44
carbon dioxide, 7, 10, 83, 85, 92
Chernobyl, 28–31, 37, 38
climate change, 7, 9, 13, 24, 29, 81, 92
coal, 9–10, 48, 56, 83
Cold War, 19
Compact Fusion Neutron Source, 79
containment building, 38, 55, 62
cooling systems, 56
cooling towers, 56, 57

DeconGel, 76
dosimeters, 40

efficiency, 25, 45, 53, 65
energy crisis, 24, 29, 52, 55, 56–57, 60, 65, 70, 81, 82, 87, 94

Fermi, Enrico, 17
fission. See nuclear fission
fission-fusion hybrid reactors, 79
fuel assemblies, 50–53, 63, 85
fuel rods, 50–53, 60, 70
Fukushima nuclear crisis, 29–31, 37, 99

graphite pebbles, 61
greenhouse gas emissions, 7, 9, 10, 13, 29, 83, 92–94

hazmat protection suits, 62
High Temperature Gas Reactor, 60–65
high-level waste, 68–70

Idaho National Laboratory, 10, 61, 97
Institute of Nuclear Power Operations, 60–61

International Atomic Energy Agency, 22

Kyoto Protocol, 92–94

Light Water Reactors, 56, 79, 98
low-level waste, 67–68, 76
  sites, 68

Manhattan Project, 18–19

neutrons, 17, 34, 47, 48, 53, 79
Next Generation Nuclear Plant, 61–65
Nuclear Energy Institute, 13, 40, 77, 85
nuclear fission, 10–13, 17, 18–19, 20, 33–34, 45, 47-48, 52, 53, 57, 62, 65, 76–77, 81, 83, 85, 86, 95
nuclear fusion, 52, 79
nuclear power plants, 7–8, 13–14, 22, 23–29, 37, 38, 40–42, 47, 50–52, 53, 55, 60–61, 67–70, 87, 94, 97, 99

construction, 22, 23–25, 28, 31, 53, 60, 89, 99
  decommissioned, 29, 70 71
  workers, 62–63
nuclear propulsion, 21
Nuclear Regulatory Commission, 25, 26, 28, 31, 39, 42, 55, 60, 68, 70, 71, 75, 89, 98

oil, 7, 9–10, 24, 56, 65, 81, 85

Power Reactor Innovative Small Modular, 77
Pressurized Water Reactor, 56–58
protests, 26, 28

radiation, 17, 19, 23, 25, 26, 28, 31, 33–45, 52, 53, 60, 62, 67–68, 70, 72, 76, 79, 95
  detection, 38, 44
  doses, 34–37, 41
  exposure, 13, 19, 31, 36–41, 72
  measuring, 36, 37
  sickness, 28, 31, 36
  types of, 34
  uses, 44

radioactive waste, 13–14, 31, 38–39, 44, 60, 62, 65, 67–79, 84–85, 91, 95
  storage, 14, 31, 62, 65, 68–70, 71, 72, 75–77, 84–85, 91
  types, 67–70
refueling, 21, 62–63, 94
renewable energy sources, 9, 91, 94
reprocessing, 42, 68, 71, 77, 79, 85, 94

safety, 13, 20, 22, 23, 25, 28–29, 39, 42, 60–61, 65, 68, 87–89, 94
SCINTIREX, 44
small modular reactors, 98
spent fuel, 31, 42, 55, 62–63, 68, 70, 71, 75, 77, 85, 94, 95
  dry casks, 70, 77
  pools, 31

TerraPower TP-1, 95
terrorism, 42
thorium, 95
Three Mile Island, 25–26, 31, 38, 60, 99
Tyvek, 62

Union of Concerned Scientists, 24
uranium, 8, 10, 17, 42, 45, 47–50, 53, 61, 64, 77, 81–82, 83, 86–87, 89, 94, 95
  mining, 10, 48–50, 83, 86–87, 89
  ore, 8, 50, 89
  pellets, 10, 50, 53
  processing, 8, 50, 89
US Department of Energy, 48, 50, 72, 75, 82, 89, 97, 98–99
  Office of Nuclear Energy, 89, 97–98

XEDOR, 53

yellowcake, 50
Yucca Mountain, 71–75

zero emissions technology, 10

ABOUT THE AUTHOR

Marcia Amidon Lusted is the author of more than sixty-five books and 250 magazine articles for young readers. She is also an assistant editor for Cobblestone Publishing's six magazines for kids, a writing instructor, and a musician. She lives in New Hampshire.

ABOUT THE CONTENT CONSULTANT

Paul Wilson is a professor of engineering physics at the University of Wisconsin–Madison, where he also received his PhD in nuclear engineering and engineering physics. His fields of interest include nuclear fuel cycles, reactor design and analysis, and energy policy. He has been recognized by the American Nuclear Society and North American Young Generation in Nuclear for his research and work in nuclear energy. Wilson is also chair of the Energy Analysis and Policy program at the university, which provides graduate students with knowledge and skills to enter professions in energy-related fields.

Medway Public Library
26 High Street
Medway, MA 02053